the complete guide to

buying
property
in Florida

THE REAL FLORIDA SPECIALISTS

Wherever in Florida you're thinking of buying a property - whether for your own personal use, to generate rental income or purely as an investment - World Property Centre can help.

With over 10 years' experience in Florida property sales, investments and management, World Property Centre can help you to realise your dream - and to make a return on your investment.

World Property Centre is a truly international company, with long-established offices both in the UK and in Florida and Canada. A complete 'one stop shop' for all your property requirements, we can not only find you the property of your dreams but also have a number of other Group divisions, each staffed by experts in the fields of:

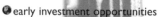

- early investment opportunities
- visa, immigration and relocation services
- business and commercial property sales
- licensed mortgage brokerage
- property rental services (with guaranteed rental services on some developments)
- title and trust services
- resort management services and property management
- foreign exchange services
- interior design services.

We currently have lots of properties in and around Florida - and on Disney's doorstep!

The property specialists you **can trust**

For more information, visit us at Stand N38 at A Place in the Sun Live, 30 September - 2 October 2005, ExCel, London and WIN the chance for a FREE Florida holiday*

Call us on 01268 286500 or visit www.worldpropertycentre.com

For distribution in the UK only.   * No purchase necessary. Terms and Conditions apply.

the complete guide to

buying property
in Florida

charles davey

**KOGAN
PAGE**

Publisher's note
Every possible effort has been made to ensure that the information contained in this book is accurate at the time of going to press, and the publishers and authors cannot accept responsibility for any errors or omissions, however caused. No responsibility for loss or damage occasioned to any person acting, or refraining from action, as a result of the material in this publication can be accepted by the editor, the publisher or any of the authors.

First published in Great Britain in 2005

Kogan Page Limited
120 Pentonville Road
London N1 9JN
United Kingdom
www.kogan-page.co.uk

© Charles Davey, 2005

ISBN 0 7494 4340 5

British Library Cataloguing in Publication Data

A CIP record for this book is available from the British Library.

Typeset by Saxon Graphics Ltd, Derby
Printed and bound in Great Britain by Thanet Press Ltd, Margate

Contents

Dreams to Reality

Founded in 1988 and directed by Alan and Hazel Bell, **The Florida Connection Ltd** is the UK's oldest Florida Property Company. With a worldwide client base this is a company that has proven experience to take care of your every need. Their services include, property management, letting, furniture packages, legal advice, immigration planning, accountancy services and Florida travel advise, they will also link you with mortgage experts.

A great annual climate, restaurants, theme parks and beautiful beaches, all make the Sunshine State a holidaymakers dream. **The Florida Connection** offers a vast selection of homes in Orlando/Kissimmee as well as the Gulf Coast.

Orlando/Kissimmee - 70 million people visit Florida annually. Over the past 12 months property prices have risen steadily and are predicted to continue throughout the year making it an ideal investment opportunity. Investment homes start at circa $300,000 (£167,000) to $500,000 (£278,000).

The Gulf Coast - a popular area, although many regions are expensive and do not allow short-term rentals.

Buying with **The Florida Connection** means the whole process is simplified yet personalised throughout. You need not even visit Florida, many clients buy this way following a visit to their UK office in Crawley Sussex. An informal meeting will answer all your questions and explain the process of purchasing and letting a home in Florida. They will be there with advice and guidance in the years after your purchase.

Now is the best time to buy Due to the excellent exchange rate currently £1=$1.80 and lowest mortgage rates for many years, there is no time like the present to invest. The fabulous climate that draws millions of visitors means that your investment will attract potential customers throughout the year.

If you feel that buying in Florida is for you then contact Alan Bell who will prepare a financial report showing exactly how much is required for the purchase followed by an itemised breakdown of running expenses and predicted income.

Dreams to Reality

The Florida Connection has helped countless people to achieve their investment dreams over the years. They are only a telephone call away. See the quality of our properties on our advert on page vii.

To turn your Dreams into Reality call The Florida Connection today on
01293 615034 or email floridaconnection@talk21.com

Preface

Florida is an ideal location for so many reasons: the climate, the beaches, the protected national parks, the tourist resorts, and for English speakers the language. Millions of people visit Florida, especially north Americans and Europeans, and many decide to purchase a holiday home there, with the Canadians and British being the most numerous after the Americans. A recent development is the rapid increase in people moving to Florida not to retire there, but to live and work there, foreigners as well as Americans.

For the British, the combination of the steep rise in the UK property market, the relatively low price of property in Florida and a favourable exchange rate has meant that many Britons can now contemplate not only the purchase of a home in Florida, but also investing in a business in Florida and thereby becoming entitled to an E-2 visa enabling them to stay almost indefinitely. There are an estimated 500,000 Britons living in Florida, with a substantial rise in the numbers over the past four years.

In the past five years the property market in Florida has experienced a boom, with prices rising by over 20 per cent per annum in certain areas of Miami, Hollywood, Fort Lauderdale, Palm Beach, West Palm Beach, Stuart, Vero Beach and even to the north in Jacksonville. Waterfront properties remain the most sought after. Hotels have been reconverted into apartments and older buildings are being demolished.

It is all too easy, however, to fall into the trap that as Florida is English-speaking, the rules and regulations governing property purchases mirror those in the UK. This is not the case. There are certain rules, regulations and practices that the prospective buyer should be aware of. Only by knowing and adhering to these can you be best protected against a purchase that could ultimately result in serious financial losses and possibly costly, lengthy and difficult court proceedings. The peaceful holiday or retirement home or, worse still, your principal residence, could turn into a veritable nightmare.

Anyone contemplating buying a house or home in Florida needs to have a basic knowledge of the process. I have endeavoured to give a precise step-by-step guide in understandable English for the prospective purchaser. I use the legal terminology, with a clear explanation of the meanings of terms used throughout the book, to make the information here accessible to all.

As a practising barrister, I am familiar with advising clients after a disaster has occurred. It is my hope and intention to guide the prospective purchaser away from the pitfalls ahead so that this situation does not occur. To this end I have placed the emphasis very much on practical advice and guidance.

This book deals with the nitty-gritty of buying or renting a home in Florida, and provides practical advice on living in Florida. It is designed to guide you through the legal labyrinth of jargon, and the general information necessary for the prospective purchaser. It is not a tourist guide. Rather, this book concentrates on the important aspects of acquiring a home there, on the practical issues pertinent to purchasing and renting a property and settling in Florida, either as a regular seasonal visitor or as a permanent resident. Where other books advise a particular course of action (such as renting before you buy), this book goes one step further by telling you how to do it.

This book aims to guide you through the main issues to help facilitate your acquisition of a house in Florida, how to make a home there, and how to avoid the mistakes that others have made.

Thinking of buying in Central Florida?

We can all dream.

Florida – the sunshine state, palm trees, sun-drenched beaches, exotic wildlife and the home of earth's gateway to the stars and Central Florida the World's entertainment capital with so much to see from DisneyWorld® & Universal Studios ® to the awe of Sea World ®. No wonder Central Florida is the place to dream… the ideal place to choose your home in the sun.

But how do you make your dream come true?
Buying in another country can seem a daunting prospect. *"How do I take the first step?"*, *"What's the right location?"*, *"How do I make the most of my investment and protect it while I am away?"*
First thing to remember is that you will not be alone. Over 50,000 Britons own a home in Florida, The market in the past 5 years has grown explosively and with strong domestic as well as overseas demand from buyers this shows no signs of slowing. In addition growing numbers of holidaymakers visiting the area on vacation choose a villa holiday.

So where to start?
Remember that any property (except "for sale by owner") in Florida can only legally be sold through a person who has an active real estate licence - ask to see the licence. To get the professional and independent advice you need we recommend that you choose a licensee who is a member of the National Association of Realtors®, and one independent from the property developer.
As with any property purchase, choosing the right villa for you and in the right location is vital. To achieve this Florida Independent Villas Inc., CEO – Peter Smith –recommends that when considering a home in the sunshine state you address three key areas;

1) Ensure you understand your primary reason for buying:
- A quick return in the current high growth Florida property market?
- A holiday home - in which case you need to consider, size of family, interests like golf, fishing etc?

- A home that will attract good rental income as well as good capital growth, in which case location is vital?

"Understanding your goals is critical and will help the Realtor® identify the right location and type of property" says Peter.

2) Fully understand the buying process..

- Understand your total financial commitment and the timing requirement for funds
- When and what contracts you will sign?
- What is a "Good Faith Estimate" and a HUD statement?
- What's the best mortgage, Sterling or Dollar, fixed or variable rate, interest only or full repayment?

"This is the area where so many people have problems. The Realtor can guide you through this process, but make sure that you fully understand what your commitments are to avoid disappointment".

3) Ensure that your investment is safe

- Key is a reliable management company to help you with the set up of your new home and look after it whilst you are away.

Peter says *"The best advice I can give to find the right management company, who will really care for your home is to purchase only through a Realtor® who will also manage it. This will ensure a level of ongoing commitment and build a successful relationship".*

It's not as daunting as it may at first seem. So once you have made your decision to buy, visit Central Florida and work with your Realtor® to view locations that meet your criteria. Let your Realtor® guide you through the buying process and you will soon be enjoying the fantastic weather and sheer excitement of Central Florida from your own home.

Peter Smith holds an active Real Estate Licence and is a member of the National Association of Realtors® can be reached at
- peter@floridaindependentvillas.com

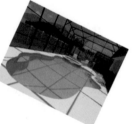

Do You Dream of Owning a Home in Florida?

Joy and Simon Bryan-Smith's dream of owning a holiday home in Florida started back in 1988 when they first visited the Sunshine State. They finally realised that dream in November 2002 when they turned the key in the door of their fabulous brand new golf course villa with a private pool.

Choosing the location of their home, picking the floor plan, deciding on the furniture and obtaining a mortgage had all been relatively simple, along with the help of their Realtor during a 5 day inspection visit to Florida back in the February of 2002. What hadn't been so easy were the several months that followed while they were waiting for their house to be built. Being 4,000 miles away, combined with the 5-hour time difference with no one experienced on hand locally to answer all those questions that the TV programmes don't cover, was what made that waiting period difficult.

- How do you find out about the various taxes which you maybe liable for? Do you have to pay income tax, and what about council tax? And what's this Tourist and Development Tax? Most importantly, how do I make sure I don't fall foul of the taxation requirements?
- If I own a property, how often can I go there? Do I need a Visa? If I own property can I retire there?
- Do I need a Bank Account in Florida? If so how do I transfer my deposit money into US Dollars at the best rate?
- How much can I expect to pay for my utility bills? How do I pay those? Do I need to set up Direct Debits?
- How will it all come together once the villa is completed? Who arranges for the utilities to be turned on? How will my furniture be delivered? Do I need to be in Florida for the Closing? And what exactly is involved in the 'Closing'?

These are just a few of the many questions which Joy and Simon pondered over during those summer months of 2002, but after many calls to Florida and several restless nights, everything worked out great...but it did set them thinking...How much easier it could all have been!

Joy and Simon both worked full time and were at the stage in life where they wanted to retire and spend more quality time together, but not put their feet up completely. Following their own experience of purchasing a property abroad, combined with the number of friends and work colleagues who had so many questions, they decided there was a niche in the market for the type of service they could offer. It was at that stage they started to put their plans into action, take early retirement from their 'real' jobs, and became Florida Real Estate Consultants here in the UK. Using the knowledge they have gained along with their Financial Services and UK Property Sales backgrounds, working in conjunction with a small team of Realtors in Florida, they now provide advice and support to anyone considering a Florida investment.

Whilst Joy and Simon are Midlands based, they take part in exhibitions all over the country, where their stand displays photos, floor plans and prices of current developments, both in and around the Disney Area, but also on the Gulf and Atlantic Coasts. They are supported by their Sons, Simon who helps out at major exhibitions, and Blake playing an important role in the background, taking calls at home, and managing e mail enquiries from their website while they are away.

It isn't just new developments that Joy and Simon deal with, there is also a vibrant second hand property market, known in America as the resale market. A resale property is becoming increasingly popular with UK citizens, as the time from viewing to Closing is usually between 6 to 8 weeks. The benefits are that you can take full advantage of the current weak US Dollar, the developments are usually completed and established and you don't have to wait for your property to be built. As many of these properties are holiday rental homes, the price you pay usually includes the furniture package too, so that your property is ready to rent out as soon as you Close, and in many cases there are already bookings in place. Joy and Simon can provide you with details of properties, which may meet your requirements and your budget, and their Realtor can arrange viewings if you have an inspection visit planned. If you are familiar with the areas and developments, as with all properties, and with the help of Joy and Simon, you can complete your purchase here in the UK without making the trip abroad.

Alternatively, deciding on a new build property also has its advantages. Apart from choosing your plot, model of home and all of those personal interior touches, including the furniture, in most cases a 10% deposit in the first month is your only outlay until the property is completed.

As with all Realtors in Florida, the team that Joy and Simon work with are all independently licensed and strictly regulated. The property sales market differs to that in the UK, in that any Realtor is able to sell you any new or resale property in the State, unlike here, where if you see a property for sale with a specific Builder, or Estate Agent, you have to deal solely with that organisation. This makes it so much easier for potential purchasers in Florida, who can work with the team of their choice, who are working on their behalf. The purchaser can also rest assured that they are not going to be charged for any service they receive from Joy and Simon in the UK or in Florida by the Realtor. In the case of all properties, whether they are a new build, or a resale property, the Seller, be that an individual or a Builder pays the sales commission, which is split between all parties involved in the sale.

As the majority of property sales to UK citizens are for the holiday market, all developments or individual houses you will be shown are on sub-divisions zoned for the short-term rental market.

So.........if you are considering whether a Florida Investment is for you, Joy and Simon can share information on actual annual costs, the buying process, financing, taxation, and tips on renting out your home. If you decide you too would like to 'live the dream' they can help arrange an inspection trip, and organise for one of their Realtors to take you around developments and properties which suit your requirements. If you like what you see, then the Florida Team can arrange everything from a Mortgage, to opening a Bank Account and setting up a Management Company to look after your home while you are not there. When you return to the UK then Joy and Simon are back on hand to deal with all of those other questions that you may have, and to ensure a smooth path to your Florida Dream.

Contact Joy and Simon Bryan-Smith 02476 388439 or 07885 627451
Or take a look at our Website www.americandreamscometrue.co.uk
E Mail info@americandreamscometrue.co.uk

Florida Villas Independent Company is a family owned business. Elethea and John Darren O'Donnell formed their own business in Florida after many successful years with property in the U.K. After buying their first Florida property they realised you get a lot more value for your money than in the U.K. or in any other countries real estate.

Besides being a holiday home, the investment and rentals is very favourable compared to most holiday destinations in regard of a potential yearly rental period. Never missing an opportunity to expand their property portfolio and knowing the rental market property inside out, they understand what attracts consumers and this is crucial if rentals are needed. They are now looking to buy their fourth home.

The rental success of their first villa prompted the company who built their home into requesting help for other buyers who wanted advice, and also for people who were already owners and had not back up from their own realtors. Providing this advice on marketing made them aware some owners, after buying a villa, the care and support was non existent, or vastly overrated or on some schemes they did not have total control over their own villa and finances. This decided them to set up their own company and join forces with Terry Teaman Vacation Homes Incorporated. Terry Teaman lives in Florida and is a licensed realtor who is very knowledgeable on vacation homes, builders, and the type of homes they build. Another very important factor is that he owns and runs his won Property Management Firm.

After buying the right location the property management is the next if not the most important issue. It provides support in the respect that your villa is looked after when your are not there, it gives peace of mind. If you need to supplement your running costs and require rentals, your clients are greeted with a villa that is beautifully cleaned and presented and any problems they may encounter will be dealt with efficiently and speedily by the management service. This ensures repeat bookings and referrals.

The Florida Villas Independent is a professional company and Elethea and Darren are also licensed broker and salesperson but it is still based from an owner's perspective and first hand knowledge of owning vacation homes. All the staff operates a friendly, no pressure, relaxed and informative method without making false and inaccurate statements or predictions. This allows you to evaluate and make your decision without being forced or coerced into making a decision just to obtain a sale. They hold the key to unlock your own dream of a successful holiday home in the sun.

FLORIDA VILLAS INDEPENDENT
41 BRISTOW CLOSE, WESTBROOK,
WARRINGTON, WA5 8EU
01925 714250

Florida

Whether you are looking for a second home in the sun, or a buy-to-let investment, few destinations can offer such great value for money, year round sunshine, as well as the fabulous diversity of Florida.

Whilst overseas buyers are spoilt for choice with a booming range of countries to choose from, the Sunshine State continues to attract a growing number of investors.

Low interest rates, excellent exchange rates and a recent high level of capital appreciation make this a prime time for buying.

A major focus for the buy-to-let investor continues to be areas close to the theme parks near Orlando. 'Demand for properties here is high.' explains Carole Saunders of Sunshine State Properties 'The popularity of Central Florida as one of the major tourist destinations in the world is looking set to rise steadily for the foreseeable future and rental incomes are strong. Low mortgage interest rates, together with a favourable exchange rate level has made property extremely attractive to overseas buyers. A combination of excellent value for money coupled with a potential for strong rental income well into the future has resulted in a high demand which is showing no signs of easing.'

'The range of properties available gives a wide choice to buyers whatever their budget.' Carole continues 'Whether you are looking for a condo, a million dollar mansion or anything in-between. At the high end of the price range for buy-to-let homes is the fabulous Reunion resort – with 3 golf courses, a $15 million dollar water park, main street, shops, restaurants and an equestrian centre – all planned for use of Reunion owners and their guests. Outside Reunion, there's a wide range of detached villas with pools to fit most budgets. More recently, condominium resorts have become extremely popular as these combine the benefits of 3-5 star hotels with individual property ownership.'

If you are looking for property outside of the Orlando area, then one up-and-coming hot spot for overseas investors is the **New Smyrna Beach** area at Central Florida's East coast.

New Smyrna is a small historic town with lots of charm close to the northern end of the Canaveral National Seashore Park. With over 13 miles of pure white beach by the Atlantic ocean this is beachside living at its finest. Palm trees border the main street at Flagler Avenue with its boutique shopping, surf shops and superb restaurants. Although prices are rising quite rapidly, two bedroom condos with beach views can still be found at under $400,000.

As Carole of Sunshine State Properties points out 'New Smyrna has traditionally been a popular holiday destination for those living in the U.S. However, international holidaymakers and investors have now discovered what a gem New Smyrna is and the market here is growing. It is the closest beach to the Orlando theme parks, with over 13 miles of beach so there is a tremendous emphasis on watersports and boating. Some of the homes and condos come complete with their own boat dock. Whether you want to sail, surf, or just relax by the beach this little piece of paradise offers it all. With Sanford Airport just over half an hour's drive away, it is easily accessible to the international traveller.'

If you prefer calmer seas then a property close to the azure waters on the **Gulf of Mexico** might be more to your taste. Whether you are looking for world class shopping, historic downtown areas, golfing, boating round the gently flowing waterways, or enjoying fabulous beaches, Florida's Gulf coast provides an idyllic backdrop for those who want to live the Florida dream.

'At the northern end of the area that we cover in Sunshine State Properties, is Manatee County' Carole continues 'including Bradenton and the barrier islands of Longboat Key and Anna Maria Island. Sarasota is just a short distance south of this, and if you like the idea of combining a coastal lifestyle with the theatre, art festivals, antiques and collectibles shops and great international restaurants, then this area may be worth putting

on your shortlist. Head South again, and you'll come to Venice, a cozy seaside town full of old world charm. The quaint downtown area here combines the best of past and present. At the southern end of our area is Charlotte county. Here you'll find a huge range of wildlife and a casual, friendly atmosphere'.

To help you realise your dream, Sunshine State Properties can help you every step along the way. 'Discussing your thoughts with one of our staff can help you to focus your ideas and turn them into a workable plan' Carole says 'we will then work with you to help you to turn those ideas into a reality. With advice and information on the buying process; mortgages; costs; properties; furnishings; different locations and the full range of information you will need. By the time our associates meet you in Florida you will have the knowledge that you need to smooth the way to your dream home. If at any time you have any questions at all, just call us either in the UK or in Florida, and we will be pleased to help. If you are intending to rent out your property, we also have UK and US rental programmes in place.'

So weather you're looking for lots of sunshine, a laid back lifestyle, sun, sea and don't forget those theme parks – Florida's charms are pretty hard to beat.

Contact:
Carole Saunders
Sunshine State Properties Ltd.
Tel: 01344 752358
Email: sales@sunshinestateproperties.co.uk

TIME10 VILLA WEBSITES

When you spend so much on a beautiful villa, you need to show it off to the world. A good villa website is the best way to turn an enquiry into a booking. We specialise in high quality but very affordable villa websites that give the information and photos your customers want to help them decide to book your property.

Our villa websites are fast loading, functional, attractive and of course individual to your property. Our standard sites come with a booking enquiry page and we have options for online booking and virtual tours.

Contact Tim Sharp
on 01677 470014

email tim@time10.com

TIME10 website
www.time10.com/villa

We have been in the web design business for over 7 years doing e-commerce sites. We take care of everything, explaining in plain English - what we are providing for you and what we need from you.

The villa featured in these images is our own, which you can of course book for your inspection trip at www.192villa.com – we'll even give you a discount if you quote "BPIF 2006".

Once you've bought your dream home, a villa website supports all the marketing that you do to get rentals. It has much more information than you can cram into printed leaflets, can be updated easily when you change things and is the single most important way that people can get a feel for your house and make that all important decision to rent yours instead of someone else's.

TIME10's Tim Sharp has been a web designer since 1996, specialising in mail order websites for small businesses. Since his family bought their house in Florida in 2004 using Dolby Properties, he's also been doing websites for villas all over the Disney Orlando area as well as the new online booking website for Alpha Florida Vacations management. On his last trip to Orlando, Tim did a dozen virtual tours using new equipment and software that produces spherical panoramas where you can look all around a room, and up and down!

You can contact Tim on **01677 470014** or by email at **tim@time10.com** or visit the website **www.time10.com/villa**

Also available from Kogan Page in *The Complete Guide to...* series:

The Complete Guide to Buying Property Abroad
fourth edition, Liz Hodgkinson

The Complete Guide to Buying Property in France
third edition, Charles Davey

The Complete Guide to Buying Property in Italy
Barbara McMahon

The Complete Guide to Buying Property in Spain
Charles Davey

The Complete Guide to Buying and Renting Your First Home
third edition, Niki Chesworth

The Complete Guide to Buying and Selling Property
second edition, Sarah O'Grady

The Complete Guide to Living and Working in Spain
Charles Davey

The Complete Guide to Letting Property
fifth edition, Liz Hodgkinson

The Complete Guide to Renovating and Improving Your Property
Liz Hodgkinson

The above titles are available from all good bookshops. To obtain further information, please contact the publisher at the address below:

Kogan Page
120 Pentonville Road
London N1 9JN
Tel: 020 7278 0433
Fax: 020 7837 6348
www.kogan-page.co.uk

THE UNITED STATES OF AMERICA

1 Welcome to Florida

The modern Florida

Florida means a 'feast of flowers'. With its semi-tropical climate it has lush all-year-round vegetation with flowers constantly in bloom, and a thriving agricultural sector including orchards of citrus fruits, sugar cane, forests for timber and winter vegetables. Its weather and its natural and artificial resources have made it a number one tourist destination, a major factor in its prosperous low tax rate economy. Indeed tourism is the mainstay of the Florida economy, with about 70 million visitors per year, generating over $50 billion annually in taxable sales, more than $3 billion in state sales taxes and over 1 million jobs.

The Sunshine State extends over some 54,000 square miles of land (larger than England), and nearly 4,500 square miles of water. It boasts some of the most-visited tourist attractions in the world, including Disney World, Sea World, Universal Studios and the Kennedy Space Center, and has some of the best golf courses in the world.

Florida is some 450 miles from north to south (St. Mary's river to Key West), and 361 miles wide (from the Atlantic Ocean to the Perdido River). To drive from Pensacola to Key West you will cover a distance of nearly 800 miles. Whilst you will find no mountains to climb (the highest natural point is only 345 feet above sea level), Florida boasts over 660 miles of beaches, 4,500 islands of more than 10 acres and nearly 8,000 lakes, the largest of which, Lake Okeechobee, is 700 square miles!

Administratively Florida is divided into 67 counties, varying in size from the tiny Union county (245 square miles) to Palm Beach (over five times larger at 2,500 square miles). It has a population of a little over 17 million people, the fourth most populated state after New York, California and Texas. The state capital is the city of Tallahassee (pop. around 150,000), but over 20 per cent of the population of Florida (nearly 4 million people) live in the metropolitan area of Miami–Fort Lauderdale.

The seven largest cities in the state are Jacksonville (pop. 750,000), Miami (pop. 365,000), Tampa (pop. 310,000), St. Petersburg (pop. 250,000), Hialeah (pop. 230,000), Orlando (pop. 190,000) and Fort Lauderdale (pop. 155,000). Six other cities have populations over 100,000.

Visitors

A high proportion of European visitors arrive at Miami airport, one of the world's busiest airports. A much smaller number fly into Fort Lauderdale airport, though it also has a high volume of traffic with plans for a new runway. At Miami you are likely to face some delays progressing through immigration control and customs control.

If you are renting a car at Miami, note that the car rental area is not the safest. Indeed criminals know that rented cars are often driven by tourists and accordingly rental cars are often a target.

It is hardly surprising that Florida is the destination of choice for many Britons and Canadians seeking to purchase a second home abroad. The Sunshine State enjoys over 300 days of sunshine a year, and an average temperature of around 21°C (70°F). Wherever you choose to holiday or to live in Florida, sea and sandy beaches are never very far away. This glorious state is packed with natural unspoilt beauty, and a vast range of tourist attractions. Despite its popularity, despite the tourists, visitors are struck by a sense of 'room to move', and an abundance of land on which to build and properties to purchase, in most areas at prices far below what you would have to pay in the UK especially. What is more, you do not even have to learn to speak another language to be able to communicate with others on an equal footing. Hardly surprising that so many northern Americans, Britons and Canadians, of all backgrounds, take to Florida like fish to water. On the subject of 'fish', note that if you see the word 'dolphin' on a restaurant menu it is referring to a tasty white fish!

It is estimated that there are about 500,000 British residents. Whilst this falls far short of the number of Britons in Spain, it is over three times the number estimated to be living in France. The Canadians are probably here in even greater numbers, with a large population from the coldest provinces – Ontario and French-speaking Quebec – and a much smaller but still significant representation from France itself. Many of these French speakers do not speak fluent English. Even more than the British they have developed their own networks and communities, including their own press. *Quoi faire en Floride* (website **www.quoifaireenfloride.net**), for example, is now in its 15th year, and contains adverts from those seeking to target Canadian French speakers in Florida, including lawyers, doctors, health clinics, dentists, real estate agencies, computer repair outlets, bars and restaurants.

Other nationalities are present here too, including Germans and Italians, and north Europeans. In many cases they choose to live in estates primarily housing those of their own nationality.

Despite the pre-eminence of English, Florida, especially southern Florida, is in many ways extremely cosmopolitan. Miami is one of the country's main ports of entry for immigrants, most notably Spanish speakers from Central and South America. Florida's Hispanic past made it a natural refuge for many of the thousands of Cubans who have left their homes since Castro came to power. Hispanics make up nearly one-fifth of the population of Florida, though as the majority live in southern Florida, the proportion is far higher there. In addition to the new arrivals, there are many residents of Florida with Spanish roots and names, often dating back several generations. Florida was, after all, under Spanish control for well over 200 years, rather longer than the period it has been part of the United States (about 100 years less).

The areas most popular with the British are the areas around Fort Lauderdale and Tampa Bay, though you will find Britons in most parts of Florida, many of whom are only too happy to welcome you to Florida and offer advice and information. There are numerous British clubs and associations, details of which are contained in this book, but about which you will find more information on one of the several websites devoted to this task, including **www.sunnybrits.com**, **www.floridabritsclub.com** and that of the British consulate in Miami, **www.britainusa.com/Miami**.

The special relationships

It is often said that the UK and the United States have a special relationship. Florida, however, has succeeded in building special relationships with both Britain and Canada, with the links with the latter being decidedly stronger and more important to Florida's economy.

It is expected that the annual number of visitors to Florida from Canada will soon exceed 2 million per annum, with the number of British visitors being around 1.5 million. Not only is Canada Florida's single most important source of foreign tourists, it is Florida's most important trading partner and single most important source of foreign investment.

A large proportion of the Canadian visitors are 'snowbirds' – primarily the retired or partially retired who spend substantial periods during the winter in warmer climates. The Canadian Snowbird Association is estimated to have around 70,000 members, a substantial majority of whom prefer Florida. Canadians who come to Florida are mainly from Ontario and French-speaking Quebec (inhabitants of western Canada tend to prefer Arizona, California, Texas and Hawaii).

Snowbirds frequently opt for destinations away from the most popular and busy tourist resorts, including much of the Panhandle (especially around Panama City), Fort Lauderdale (Hollywood Beach is particularly popular with French-speaking Canadians), and southwestern Florida, in the area running roughly from Punta Gorda to Naples. The snowbirds are attracted by more modest house prices, lower crime rates and the more relaxed lifestyle in the Panhandle and the southwest coast, than to the busier southeast coast. Estimates of the number of Canadians owning property in Florida vary from 100,000 to 500,000 (if timeshares are counted). To be added to that figure is the substantial number of Canadians staying in trailer parks.

West Realty is a full service real estate company working in and around Orlando Florida.

We specialize in second home sales and as members of the National Association of Realtors, Florida association of Realtors, and Osceola county Association of Realtors, you can feel confident with our ethical business practices.

All our agents are skillful negotiators who have expert knowledge of the area. They are trained to handle both residential as well as vacation home sales and people who are looking to relocate.

We work frequently with International and out of state buyers and have helped many people make the move to Florida. We can assist in every step, from opening a bank account, finding a mortgage, and of course helping to find your ideal home. Once you purchase your dream home that is only the beginning. We are here with support before, during and after your purchase.

Vacation Rental Homes

If you are purchasing a vacation rental home, our agents will assist you by putting you in touch with a reputable management team. We work closely with many companies that can help to offset the costs with weekly rentals of your vacation/ holiday home. A property manager will take care of the lawn, pool, pest control, and rentals if you are looking to offset the costs.

Residential Property

Whether you are looking to purchase a new or resale property our agents can help to locate your dream home. We work closely with some of Florida's most reputable builders and can help locate a home in one of the new subdivisions, put you in touch with a custom builder or help you find a cozy condo. As members of the National Association of Realtors we work with a network of realtors across the State of Florida and can help you to find information on almost any home for sale in Florida.

Private Vacation Homes

If the home you purchase is a private vacation home. Our in-house West Realty Management team can help to insure that your home away from home is being well looked after when it is not being used. We offer services with a personal touch. Your home will be monitored and maintained to a high standard and we insure plenty of regular feedback from our well-trained staff.

Booking Agency

West Realty has also teamed up with a successful booking agency who can help to get you additional bookings for your home should you wish to rent it out. We will provide you with a Free Virtual Tour of your home which will be placed on our booking agency site.

SERVICES WEST REALTY PROVIDES

Buyers Services

- Helping you to find the most suitable property.
- Handling the legal aspects of the purchase.
- Liaising with the builder or sellers agent
- Monitoring construction and taking photographs during construction.
- Financing Pre-Qualification
- Liaising with the mortgage broker and ensuring the final paperwork is in order.
- Carrying out the pre-occupation inspection, coordinating the delivery of furnishings and organizing the connection of all services.
- Free Virtual Tour for people purchasing a vacation rental home. This will help you to market your property for rentals.
- No Cost for Buyers Services

Management Services

- Specializing in the care of Private Vacation Homes
- Trained Staff who maintain your home regularly
- Monthly Update to inform you about the status of your home
- Lawn care
- Pool Maintenance
- Cleaning Services
- On site Management Staff to oversee your home

Booking Agency

- Providing additional bookings for your rental property
- Marketing your home throughout Europe and the US
- Your Virtual Tour will be uploaded on our booking agency website
- Free Consultation for tips to help make your home stand out from others on the rental market

Visit our website to view properties for sale throughout Florida
www.westrealtyorlando.com or call 0800-389-2875

FLORIDA

2 Choosing your location

Once you have decided to purchase a holiday or retirement home in Florida you will need to narrow your property search down to certain areas. There is a wide diversity and considerable care is required before coming to a decision. Although property prices are generally much lower than in the UK (with notable exceptions on the southeast and southwest coasts), the costs of purchasing are still high. If you make a mistake and have to sell and change areas this will be costly. You may also have difficulties in selling as quickly as you would have wished. I strongly recommend that you rent first to avoid making expensive and time-consuming mistakes. You can take your time getting to know your area at your leisure and, indeed, visit other areas within easy reach, before making a decision that can affect your life positively or negatively for many years to come.

In deciding where to start, it is a good idea to list the factors that are important to you. These are likely to include many of the following.

Climate

In Florida the summers are hot wherever you are, with only a degree or two of difference between the north and the south. Winters, on the other hand, are significantly warmer (10–15 degrees) in the south. Coastal properties have the advantage of sea breezes, whereas inland you might find it stiflingly hot. The geography is very different from that of the French Riviera or the Costa del Sol, where inland areas are mountainous and provide residents with a cool refreshing break from the heat in the hot summers. Florida is definitely very flat. While geographical location is important, ensure also that the property you buy faces the sun – in particular (if appropriate) its main balconies, terraces and gardens.

Property prices and the cost of living

There are so many different factors that determine property prices that it is unwise to over-generalize about different regions. Much depends on a property's exact location within a region, its proximity to local facilities and communication routes, its condition and the views – to mention only some of the matters that influence price. Even the condition of the neighbouring property may have a very significant effect on the price of the property for sale. It is safe to say, however, that the cheapest properties are those in rural areas, particularly the least populated, while coastal areas tend to be among the most popular and most expensive. Two other general rules, subject as always to exceptions, are that northern Florida is less expensive than the south, and that the east coast tends to be more expensive than the west coast.

Employment

If you are or may become entitled to work, you may need to be within striking distance of one of the main cities. Many Britons find employment in British-run businesses, many Canadians in Canadian-run businesses. Large numbers of Britons and Canadians set up on their own providing a service to their fellow countrymen, making use of contacts established within the various expatriate groups and associations. If you are looking for employment and wish to be able to network amongst the expatriate community, you will need to choose an area popular with your fellow nationals.

Crime

Whilst major cities inevitably attract more crime, remember that remote houses can be extremely vulnerable. This is less true of rural village properties – a stranger will find their presence noted by the locals, and this discourages theft and break-ins.

Noise and pollution

Properties adjacent to motorways, airports and industrial areas tend to be cheaper for obvious reasons. Do not assume that life in the countryside is necessarily peaceful. Watch out for motorway and other road routes – both those already constructed and those planned. Nearby church bells can shatter the quiet of a Sunday morning. Even more disturbing is the presence of a cockerel (or worse still a peacock), even some distance away, keen to provide a wake-up call early every morning of every week of every year, with reminders during the day.

Tourists

Florida is one of the world's most popular tourist destinations. Remember that some areas that are relatively quiet much of the year may be overrun by tourists in the summer, and you may find yourself having to join them on grid-locked roads that resemble overflowing car parks, stifling in the heat. On the other hand, some property owners in the more popular areas can rent out their properties during the high season, charging rentals rather higher than their monthly mortgage payments.

Education

If you have children of school age, you will obviously have to choose your area with care, especially if your child is to attend a public school in which case he or she will almost certainly be attending the school nearest to the house you purchase. Guidance is available, for example in finding out different schools' examination results (see Chapter 11), though you should not underestimate the help and assistance that you may be able to obtain from other expatriates who have children of school age.

Proximity of facilities

If you are elderly or suffer from bad health you should avoid remote areas and consider settling not too far from centres of medical care. On the other hand, living a little inland, or in the Panhandle, may enable you to rent or purchase a larger property and enjoy living without the restrictions imposed on occupants of apartment blocks. You do, however, need to bear in mind the advantages of having shops, restaurants and other facilities around the corner.

The local population

The most important ingredient in settling in Florida will be your own determination to participate in the community into which you have moved. In many areas of Florida you have the choice of living almost entirely amongst fellow Britons, Canadians, Germans, Scandinavians etc, or living in a completely American world, or of opting for a middle course.

Transport links to the UK and Canada

Obviously this is very different from living in France or Spain where many routes have been opened in recent years linking provincial cities in both countries. On the other hand, Florida is rather smaller than either of these two popular European destinations, and has an excellent road network.

As far as scheduled flights from the UK are concerned, the British are limited to flights from London and Manchester. Whilst Florida has six international airports: Miami, Orlando, Tampa/St. Petersburg, Fort Lauderdale, Jacksonville and Daytona Beach, the direct flights from the UK are only to the first three of these. From Canada, there are many direct flights to Florida destinations from Toronto and Montreal, some flights from Vancouver for those living in the west of Canada, and also from other Canadian provincial cities (see Appendix 2).

There are, of course, many flights to Florida airports from both the UK and Canada with one change, often in New York, Newark or Washington, DC. Scottish residents may find it most convenient to fly via Toronto with one of the new low-cost airlines, thereby cutting out a journey to London.

In addition to scheduled flights, there are good selections of charter flights from provincial airports to Miami, Orlando and Tampa.

Availability of British and Canadian contacts, goods and services

You may wish to socialize with other Britons, whether Scots, Irish, Welsh or English, or fellow Canadians. If you do, there are numerous organizations, especially in the more popular areas. There are British and Canadian newspapers and magazines, and various stores selling British and Irish food and other products. There are also many English (and Irish) pubs scattered throughout Florida. The British consulate in Miami (**www.britainusa.com/miami**) keeps a list of British clubs and associations. See also **www.sunnybrits.com**.

Hurricanes and other natural disasters

Florida is also famous, of course, for its hurricanes which can do such devastating damage to property. This does not seemed to have dampened down enthusiasm for Florida, with estate agents (realtors) reporting that they were selling property even whilst the last hurricane was raging. Some areas of Florida also suffer from floods. Fortunately you can consult the website **www.hazardmaps.gov/atlas.php**. Here you can search for information about damage from natural disasters such as floods and hurricanes in any particular locality. The search facility will even let you search the road in which you are considering making a purchase. In some areas of Florida phosphate has contaminated water supplies. For further information see **www.thephosphaterisk.com**.

The regions of Florida

Florida is divided administratively into 67 counties, each with a county seat or capital. In the text below I have also divided Florida into different regions. I have done this for convenience, and to some extent the divisions are artificial, especially on the borders, in that there are no sharp divisions. You can find much information on each county of Florida on the website **www.floridasmart.com**, and an interactive atlas of Florida at **www.freac.fsu.edu/InteractiveCountyAtlas**.

REGIONS OF FLORIDA

COUNTIES OF FLORIDA

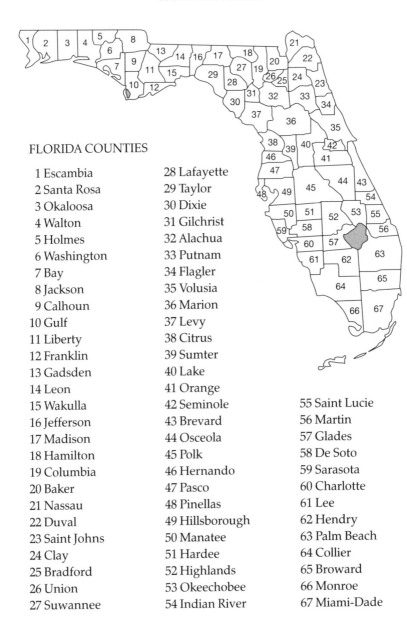

FLORIDA COUNTIES

1 Escambia
2 Santa Rosa
3 Okaloosa
4 Walton
5 Holmes
6 Washington
7 Bay
8 Jackson
9 Calhoun
10 Gulf
11 Liberty
12 Franklin
13 Gadsden
14 Leon
15 Wakulla
16 Jefferson
17 Madison
18 Hamilton
19 Columbia
20 Baker
21 Nassau
22 Duval
23 Saint Johns
24 Clay
25 Bradford
26 Union
27 Suwannee

28 Lafayette
29 Taylor
30 Dixie
31 Gilchrist
32 Alachua
33 Putnam
34 Flagler
35 Volusia
36 Marion
37 Levy
38 Citrus
39 Sumter
40 Lake
41 Orange
42 Seminole
43 Brevard
44 Osceola
45 Polk
46 Hernando
47 Pasco
48 Pinellas
49 Hillsborough
50 Manatee
51 Hardee
52 Highlands
53 Okeechobee
54 Indian River

55 Saint Lucie
56 Martin
57 Glades
58 De Soto
59 Sarasota
60 Charlotte
61 Lee
62 Hendry
63 Palm Beach
64 Collier
65 Broward
66 Monroe
67 Miami-Dade

Northwest Florida ('The Panhandle')

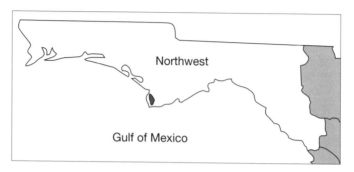

This area of Florida, known as the Panhandle, consists of a thin stretch of land, for the most part only about 40 to 50 miles wide, washed by the Gulf of Mexico and starting from the state border with Alabama, extending eastwards and then in a southerly direction as far as Cedar Key and Waccasassa Bay. It consists of the 22 counties starting from Escambia in the west, to Levy at its southern extremity, and ranging in size from 500 square miles to 1,400 square miles. All are very sparsely populated save for Escambia, Santa Rosa and Okaloosa, at the western end of the Panhandle, and Leon which contains Tallahassee, the Florida state capital. Route 98 runs from Pensacola on the western border with Alabama, along the coast as far as Tallahassee in the east, and then inland as it turns south down to Levy.

This part of Florida has four distinct seasons. The average winter temperature is around 12°C for all counties, save for the six most southern counties where the winter temperature averages around 14°C. The average summer temperature is a fairly constant 26–28°C degrees throughout the Panhandle, save for Gilchrist (inland) where the average summer temperature reaches 30°C. Most counties have an average rainfall between 50 and 60 inches a year, though notable exceptions are Levy (45 inches), Walton (66) and Washington (71).

It is often said, with good reason, that the north of Florida with its rural landscape and large plantations is characteristic of the southern states of the United States, sharing much with neighbouring Georgia and Alabama. The southern half of Florida, however, is far more cosmopolitan, with its mix of many nationalities, most notably economic immigrants, from the Caribbean, Central and South America and of course large numbers from elsewhere in the United States, Canada, the UK and other northern European countries, in search of the warm climate.

The region boasts miles of stunning beaches, the longest in Florida, but the area remains relatively undeveloped, especially the coasts of the counties of Taylor, Dixie and Levy, part of what has been termed the 'Nature Coast'. The area is noted for its fishing, and seafood. House prices in the region remain quite low. You should have no problem in finding a reasonably sized family property for under $200,000.

General websites: **www.nwfdailynews.com/index.shtml**; **www.emeraldcoast.com/**.

The counties

Escambia County (pop. 300,000; area 875 square miles; administrative capital Pensacola) **www.co.escambia.fl.us**; **www.myescambia.com**; **www.ci.pensacola.fl.us/**

The county is fairly highly populated, with many residents of Escambia, and indeed the two counties to the east, being employed at the huge Elgin Air Force Base. The administrative centre is the port of Pensacola. This historic city, with many restored buildings from years gone by, was at different times under French, Spanish and British rule. If you like music, whether the classics, jazz or contemporary, you will enjoy the free weekly evening concerts given by the Pensacola Symphony Orchestra every summer in Seville Square, where you can stretch out on the grass for a lazy evening's entertainment. Music receives strong local support, including in the form of an annual Summer Music Festival. The city hosts the Great Gulf Coast Arts Festival each year, attracting more than 200,000 people. You will also find a Museum of Art housing works of 20th-century American artists and regular exhibitions, and the Saenger Theater which regularly welcomes Broadway touring companies. There are also local ballet and opera companies. There is an Irish pub in Pensacola, McGuire's Irish Pub and Brewery, 600 East Gregory Street (tel: (850) 433 6789).

Penascola is the home of the University of West Florida (UWF), a friendly university with under 8,000 students, and class sizes averaging less than 25. Alabama's Troy State University is within a relatively short distance, and there is also a Pensacola Christian College with nearly 4,000 students annually. Over 30,000 students attend courses at Pensacola Junior College covering the arts, nursing, dental and health training, environmental sciences, agriculture, and horticulture courses.

Escambia County is also home to the **National Museum of Naval Aviation,** one of the most visited museums in Florida. It contains more than 130 carefully restored aircraft, equipment, and artefacts from the nearly 90 years of US naval history. The museum has flight simulators, and you can also visit the Cubi Café. This is a re-creation of the famous officers' club bar at Cubi Point Naval Air Station in the Philippines.

Escambia County boasts more than 30 miles of quiet beaches lapped by the warm azure blue waters of the Bay of Mexico. The beaches are of fine white sand, and are lined by a protective barrier of islands of the Gulf Islands Natural Seashore, between which you will find a host of water sporting activities including swimming, sailing and fishing. Pensacola Beach is a little noisier with its various fun activities, shops and restaurants.

Santa Rosa County (pop. 120,000; area 1,200 square miles; administrative capital Milton) **www.co.santa-rosa.fl.us; www.ssrcchamber.com**

Despite being one of the four most populated states in the Panhandle, the inhabitants of Santa Rosa County never have to travel very far to escape the traffic congestion and noise of daily life and take advantage of a wide range of recreational activities, whether on its stunning white sandy beaches, or inland in the unspoiled forests, creeks and rivers. Besides the usual range of water sports, there are ample opportunities for hiking, fishing, hunting, camping, tennis and golf.

Okaloosa County (pop. 172,000; area 1,100 square miles; administrative capital Crestview) **www.co.okaloosa.fl.us; www.destin-fwb.com**

The name of this county is thought to mean 'water' and 'black', and indeed a river named the Blackwater River does flow through this county. As in other counties along this coast, you will find miles of beautiful sandy sugar-white beaches. There is also a wide range of sporting opportunities, many based in the clear waters of the Blackwater River. The county is also home to the huge Eglin Air Force Base.

Walton County (pop. 41,000; area 1,200 square miles; administrative capital DeFuniak Springs) **www.waltoncountychamber.com**

Sparsely populated, but growing rapidly, Walton County boasts stunning beaches, including 16 Blue Wave beaches, and coastal dune lakes unique outside of Africa. Forests abound. The north has large areas devoted to agriculture. The county has one of Florida's highest points – little more than 100 metres above sea level. Inhabited by the Euchee and Creek Indians, the first European settlers were Scots. The mainstays of the local economy are timber and tourism, with over half a million people visiting the county each year, many of them regular visitors attracted by the natural beauty. In DeFuniak Springs you will find Victorian buildings constructed around a natural but completely round lake, and the oldest library in Florida. At the Chautauqua Winery, there are free tours and wine tasting. A fisherman's paradise, there is a choice between deep-sea fishing in the Gulf of Mexico, and fishing for brim or bass in the rivers off the Choctawhatchee Bay.

Holmes County (pop. 19,000; area 500 square miles; administrative capital Bonifay)
     A sparsely populated inland rural county.

Washington County (pop. 21,000; area 600 square miles; administrative capital Chipley) **www.washingtonfl.com**
     A rural inland county situated midway between Pensacola and Tallahassee. Most of the county is uninhabited.

Bay County (pop. 150,000; area 1,000 square miles; administrative capital Panama City)
     Bay County boasts the well-developed and popular coastal destination of Panama City, where house prices are a little higher than in most of the northwestern counties, with prices expected to continue to increase at an above average rate.

Jackson County (pop. 47,000; area 950 square miles; administrative capital Marianna) **www.jacksoncountyfl.com**

Calhoun County (pop. 13,000; area 570 square miles; administrative capital Blountstown) **www.calhounco.org**
     An inland county that has avoided most aspects of commercialized tourism. The area is categorized by clear springs, creeks, rivers and vast forests, home to a rich variety of wild game, fish, molluscs, tupelo honey, and many native fruits and vegetables. Attractions include the Nature Conservancy, the Torreya State Park, the Big Bend Wildlife Sanctuary and the Panhandle Pioneer Settlement. The biologically rich Apalachicola River Basin is home to at least 127 rare species of plants and animals and 45 of Florida's 62 native habitats. The Chipola River State Canoe Trail is another popular destination for tourists.

Gulf County (pop. 14,000; area 740 square miles; administrative capital Port St. Joe) www.visitgulf.com; www.gulfcountybusiness.com; www.gulfcountygovernment.com/

The beaches are stunning, with that at St. Joseph State Park being particularly noteworthy. Visitors come to Gulf County to comb the beaches, for walking, swimming, boating, fishing, kayaking, horseback riding, and the golf courses.

Franklin County (pop. 11,500; area 1,000 square miles (nearly half of which consists of lakes and rivers); administrative capital Apalachicola) www.franklincountyflorida.com; www.apalachicolabay.org – website for Franklin County Chamber of Commerce

Franklin County is southwest of Tallahassee and to the southeast of Panama City. It has some 200 miles of coastal shoreline. Kayaking is a popular sport, as are fishing, boating and biking. The county has extensive areas of primitive forests popular for hiking, hunting and fishing, as well as acres of marshland and swamps, and along the coast a series of barrier islands under the title of the St. Vincent Island National Wildlife Refuge. Cycling is popular.

Liberty County (pop. 7,000; area 850 square miles; administrative capital Bristol) www.fn1.tfn.net/Liberty_County/

Liberty is a very sparsely populated undeveloped inland county, sandwiched between the rivers Ochlockonee and Apalachicola. The northern third of the county consists of farmland, and the rest is occupied by the Apalachicola National Forest. Activities include hunting, fishing and canoeing.

Gadsden County (pop. 45,000; area 500 square miles; administrative capital Quincy)

Leon County (pop. 250,000; area 700 square miles; administrative capital Tallahassee) www.co.leon.fl.us; www.seetallahassee.com; www.tallahassee.com; www.state.fl.us/citytlh

Tallahassee is an inland city, and though much smaller than the large cities of Miami in the southeast and Jacksonville in the northeast, it is the capital of the state of Florida. Tallahassee is noted for its old-fashioned charm, its large number of historic sites and buildings, and the restored Old Capitol building and the New Capitol. The latter is worth a visit, not least for the panoramic view from the 22nd-floor observatory. Tallahassee is also an academic and cultural centre, and the home of several history museums. The county is noted for the large number of its plantations, fishing and hunting, and its unspoilt natural environment. On the coast at Apalachicola, St. George Island and Eastpoint you will find miles of beautiful beaches and shallow bays ideal for swimming.

Property prices in Tallahassee remain modest and you should be able to find a family home for around $150,000. Note that in parts of Tallahassee there are risks of flood damage. You can obtain guidance on this by consulting the website **www.state.fl.us/citytlh**. A Tallahassee Relocation Information Pack, including a Newcomer's Guide, is available from the Tallahassee Area Convention and Visitors Bureau (tel: (850) 413 9200). It contains invaluable information about resources in Leon County, including schools, health services, churches, utilities, telephone, driver's licences and voter registration.

Wakulla County (pop. 23,000; area 750 square miles; administrative capital Crawfordville) **www.wakulla.com**

Jefferson County (pop. 13,000; area 600 square miles; administrative capital Monticello)

Jefferson County is situated amongst Florida's rolling hills. It stretches from the border with Georgia in the north to the Gulf of Mexico to the south, and is about halfway between Pensacola at the most westerly part of Florida and Jacksonville on the northeast coast. The county seat, Monticello, is only 23 miles from the state capital, Tallahassee, and dates from the era of the plantations. It was popular with wealthy industrialists from the northern states, who together with the plantation owners built many majestic buildings that are now listed on the National Historic Register.

The county is crossed by the rivers Wacissa, Aucilla and St. Marks, to name but the three most important, running through forests and marshlands where tourists seldom venture. There are many lakes, including Lake Miccosukee which is over 6,200 acres. The Aucilla river is ideal for accomplished canoeists with its swift currents and rapids. Visitors also come for the hunting, which includes a plentiful supply of wild game. Wildlife reserves include the Aucilla Wildlife Management Area in the south of the county and St. Marks Wildlife Refuge on the coast.

Land and property prices are reasonable, and with its low crime rate Jefferson County is becoming increasingly popular with the retired.

Madison County (pop. 18,700; area 700 square miles; administrative capital Madison)

Madison County is inland, bordering on Georgia, and blessed with rolling hills, forests, lakes and rivers. This county gives the impression of being extremely remote, but is in fact not far from the cities of Tallahassee and Jacksonville. Popular activities include horse riding, biking, canoeing and hiking.

Taylor County (pop. 19,500; area 1,200 square miles; administrative capital Perry) **www.tcfl-libinfo.com**; **www.taylorcountychamber.com**

A coastal county, the county seat of Perry is just over 50 miles south of Tallahassee.

Lafayette County (pop. 7,000; area 550 square miles; administrative capital Mayo)

Dixie County (pop. 14,000; area 850 square miles; administrative capital Cross City) **www.dixiecounty.org**

Gilchrist County (pop. 14,500; area 360 square miles; administrative capital Trenton) **www.co.gilchrist.fl.us**

Like many of the counties in the northwest, this is a sparsely populated area and has been left relatively untouched by the growth in tourism in Florida. The famous Suwannee River flows through the west of the county. The county is also home to several of Florida's springs, including the Hart Springs, the Ginnie Springs and the Blue Springs.

Levy County (pop. 34,500; area 1,400 square miles; administrative capital Bronson)

The largest county, but with a very small population. Cedar Keys, one of the main population centres in the county, is in fact a small island village just off the coast. Not far is the Cedar Keys National Wildlife Refuge consisting of a collection of barrier islands.

Northeast Florida

The coastal stretch of this region, lapped by the Atlantic, is characterized by golden beaches, sand dunes and barrier islands. It was one of the first areas to fall under the Spanish flag, and there are several historic towns dating from this era. Economically, the region is dominated by Jacksonville, by population the largest city in Florida, and geographically one of the largest cities in the world. The average winter temperature is between 12 and 14°C for all counties, save for Alachua (10). The average summer temperature is a fairly constant 27–28°C throughout the region. Most counties have an average rainfall of between 48 and 53 inches a year, though Duval has an annual average of 58 inches of rain.

The counties

Hamilton County (pop. 13,500; area 520 square miles; administrative capital Jasper) **www.hamiltoncountyflorida.com**; **www.hamiltoncountyonline.com**

Hamilton County is a rural county on the border with Georgia. To the east and south border is the famous Suwannee River (see below), and to the west is the Withlacoochee. Hamilton resembles a peninsula within a peninsula. To the east is Jacksonville, and to the west is Tallahassee.

Suwannee County (pop. 35,000, area 700 square miles; administrative capital Live Oak) **www.liveoak.govoffice.com**; **www.suwanneechamber.com**

This county takes its name from the Suwannee River, famous for the song that is now Florida's state anthem 'Way Down Upon the Swanee River'. There is uncertainty as to the derivation of the name. One account is that it comes from the Cherokee word *Sawani*, meaning 'echo river', and another is that it is a corruption of the Spanish San Juan.

Alachua County (pop. 22,000; area 970 square miles; administrative capital Gainesville)

An inland county 50 miles from the Gulf of Mexico and 67 miles from the Atlantic Ocean. The county seat, Gainesville, is also the site of the

University of Florida, and is noted for a good selection of antique and art shops. The area is unspoilt and wild, with stunning rivers and lakes and natural springs.

Baker County (pop. 22,500; area 590 square miles; administrative capital Maccleny)
   Though quiet and tranquil, this fairly sparsely populated county is but a short drive from Jacksonville.

Bradford County (pop. 26,000; area 300 square miles; administrative centre Starke) **www.bradford-co-fla.org**

Clay County (pop. 142,000; area 650 square miles; administrative centre Green Cove Springs) **www.claycountygov.com**
   This is an economically prosperous county, just south of Jacksonville, with plenty of facilities, waterways, calm lakes and green golf courses.

Columbia County (pop. 60,000; area 797 square miles; administrative centre Lake City) **www.lakecitychamber.com**
   An inland county, on the border with Georgia and almost midway between Tallahassee and Jacksonville. The county boasts many lakes and rivers, hence the name of its administrative capital, Lake City. The rivers flowing through the county include the Suwannee, the Santa Fe and the Ichtucknee rivers. The area is noted for its water sport activities, including water-skiing. Lake City is within easy access of the Stephen Foster State Park, the Spirit of the Suwannee Music Park, the O'Lena State Park and the Olustee Beach.

Duval County (pop. 780,000; area 920 square miles; administrative capital Jacksonville)
   The city of Jacksonville, with over 700,000 inhabitants, has expanded rapidly over the past 30 years. It accounts for nearly the entire population of the county. The city is huge, occupying almost the entire county, and a total area larger than New York City, with many pleasant residential areas, and a series of waterside developments either side of St. John's river. A family home can be purchased for under $150,000. In addition to a significant commercial centre, there is also a substantial amount of industry. Fly's Tie Irish Pub is situated at 177E Sailfish Drive, Atlantic Beach. There is another Irish Pub Jacksonville Beach at 514 N First St.

There is a British club in Jacksonville. Contact Walter (904) 215 3779; **www.jacksonvillebritishclub.com**.

Flagler County (pop. 50,000; area 570 square miles; administrative capital Bunnell) **www.visitflagler.org**

Flagler County borders on the Atlantic Ocean, with stunning undeveloped beaches to the east and rural countryside inland to the west, not to mention its thick subtropical forests. There are excellent facilities for golf and tennis.

Nassau County (pop. 58,000, area 725 square miles; administrative capital Fernandina Beach) **www.nassauclerk.org**

The most northern of Florida's counties, and bordering on the Atlantic Ocean. Nassau is a prosperous county growing at an unprecedented rate.

Putnam County (pop. 71,000; area 830 square miles; administrative capital Palatka) **www.co.putnam.fl.us**

Saint John's County (pop. 125,000; area 820 square miles; administrative capital St. Augustine) **www.co.st-johns.fl.us; www.visitoldcity.com**

Bordering on the Atlantic Ocean, Saint John's County has wonderful beaches, but is most well known for its historical capital, St. Augustine, established by the Spanish as long ago as 1565 and the Castillo de San Marcos, a Spanish fortification dating from the late 17th century. The city boasts a skilfully restored Spanish quarter, where a number of the properties are officially protected sites. Care is required before buying property here, as there are strict rules in force as to what proprietors can and cannot do. Outside the Spanish quarter, you should have no problem in finding a reasonable family home for under $150,000. St. Augustine has a number of British and Irish pubs, including the King's Head, 6460 US 1 North, Lynch's Irish Pub, 32 Avenida Menendez and The White Lion, 20 Cuna Street.

Union County (pop. 13,500; area 250 square miles; administrative capital Lake Butler)

The smallest county in the state.

Central West Florida

Gulf of Mexico

Central West

This is a fast-growing region, containing the highly developed cities of Tampa, St. Petersburg, Clearwater and Bradenton. The average winter temperature is around 15°C for most of the region, with summer temperatures around 27–28°C. Average rainfall is around 55 inches, though Hillsborough is somewhat drier with an average of only 48.5. The coastline is characterized by peninsulas and barrier islands. The waters along this stretch of the coast are shallow, and always warm enough for swimming. The sand on the beaches is dazzlingly white. On the southern shore of Tampa Bay you will see a memorial to the Spanish explorer Herando de Soto – it was from here that the Spaniards began their expeditions into the central southern areas of the United States.

The counties

Citrus County (pop. 120,000; area 775 square miles; administrative capital Inverness) **www.bocc.citrus.fl.us/**

DeSoto County (pop. 32,500; area 640 square miles; administrative capital Arcadia) **www.co.desoto.fl.us**
 DeSoto County is named after the Spanish explorer Hernando de Soto.

Hernando County (pop. 133,000; area 590 square miles; administrative capital Brooksville) **www.co.hernando.fl.us**
 Hernando County is situated just to the north of Tampa Bay, on the west coast. The county forms part of The Nature Coast, and accordingly much of it falls within the Chassahowitzka National Wildlife Refuge, the Chinsegut Hill National Wildlife Refuge, the Withlacoochee State Forest, and the Weeki Wachee Preserve. There is a plentiful supply of recreational activities. Apart from championship golf, visitors come to hunt, fish, camp, hike and ride the wilderness bicycle trail.
 Whilst the county seat is at Brooksville, the largest centre is that at Spring Hill, which has a population of about 80,000, well over half the population of Hernando County. It is about 30–40 minutes' drive from Tampa.

Hillsborough County (pop. 1 million; area 1,266 square miles; administrative capital Tampa) **www.hillsboroughcounty.org**; **www.visittampabay.com**; **www.tampagov.net**; **www.introtampabay.com/**

The City of Tampa is the third most populated city in Florida, and home to around one-third of the inhabitants of Hillsborough County. It is an international port, but also has a varied economy that includes tourism, agriculture, construction, finance, health care and technology. Tampa is decidedly multicultural, with several different ethnic quarters, including Ybor City on the outskirts of Tampa, which is decidedly Cuban and fast becoming a popular residential area for younger citizens. Not surprisingly, Tampa has an important Hispanic population from a wide range of different Latin American countries, amounting to about 10 per cent of the city's population, with a much greater proportion of the inhabitants having some Hispanic blood in their family line. Tampa Bay is a lively, exciting and affluent area in which you can take full advantage of the facilities of urban life, such as its varied cultural attractions, as well as activities associated with the glorious beaches nearby and extensive waterways including the Hillsborough and Alafia rivers.

Housing is reasonably priced, and significantly lower than in Sarasota to the south. You should be able to purchase a reasonably sized family home for not much more than $150,000.

In the summer the warm temperatures are accompanied by gentle breezes and short showers, usually in the afternoon. There are a number of British and Irish pubs in Tampa (including O'Brien's Irish Pub at 11744 North Dale Mabry Highway, Mad Dogs & Englishmen at 4115 South MacDill Avenue, and MacDinton's Irish Pub and Restaurant, 405 S Howard Avenue, see **www.macdintons.com**). There is the Irish Pub in Ybor City. For a detailed list of pubs and restaurants with a British or Irish atmosphere see **www.sunnybrits.com**.

Manatee County (pop. 270,000; area 900 square miles; administrative capital Bradenton). **www.co.manatee.fl.us**

There are a couple of pubs in Bradenton (Crown & Anchor and O'Hara's).

Pasco County (pop. 350,000; area 870 square miles; administrative capital Dade City) **www.pascocountyfl.net**; **www.pascofla.com**; **www.pinellascounty.org**

Pinellas County (pop. 950,000; area 608 square miles; administrative capital Clearwater)

The county boasts a fine selection of stunning beaches, country parks, calm lakes and beautiful countryside. The St. Petersburg/Clearwater peninsula is lapped by the waters of the Gulf of Mexico to the west and by Tampa Bay to the east, and partially lined by 20 barrier islands. Whilst Pinellas is not a large county, it is one of the more populated areas of Florida. There are still a good many beaches within close proximity, though property prices are well above the state average. The city has the most extensive collection of original works by Salvador Dali. There are pubs in St. Petersburg (The Harp & Thistle Irish Pub) and Clearwater (Tommy Duff's Irish Aviation Pub and, on the beach, the Big Ben Pub).

Central Florida

In the past 30 years Central Florida has undergone development that far exceeds any other area of Florida. It has become a veritable holidaymakers' paradise! Disneyland, however, is but one of the many attractions that have been added to the region's rich and wonderful natural landscape, lakes and wildlife. That said, the opening of Disneyworld in 1971 really placed Orlando on the world map. Average winter temperatures in the region are around 15°C, with Sumter and Marion being a little cooler, and average summer temperatures around 27–28°C. Average yearly rainfall figures are around 50 inches.

The counties

Marion County (pop. 280,000; area 1,600 square miles; administrative capital Ocala) **www.marioncountyfl.org**

Marion County is the fifth largest county in Florida. The county seat Ocala is a world-renowned centre for horse breeding and training. Property prices remain amongst the lowest in Florida. Although mostly rural, much of the population is employed in industry and services.

Sumter County (pop. 54,000; area 580 square miles; administrative capital Bushnell) **www.bocc.co.sumter.fl.us**

Lake County (pop. 210,000, area 1,150 square miles; administrative capital Tavares)

Lake County is named after its large number of lakes (1,400 named lakes) which cover over 200 square miles. Compared to other counties in Florida, Lake County has quite a diverse landscape, with much of the county consisting of rolling hills, and boasting Florida's highest point (315 feet above sea level). This is a prosperous county, with the past few years witnessing a boom in the construction of new homes, many on the outskirts of the county's various small and growing towns. Lake County has a great deal of appeal for both families and sports enthusiasts, with a plentiful supply of countryside activities. Popular leisure-time pursuits include cruising on the county's lakes, and water-skiing. Canoeists and kayak practitioners will appreciate the 'blueways' – where markers guide them along a trail through the county's extensive network of waterways. The blueways are supported by water-borne emergency and rescue teams. There is also a nationally accredited triathlon training centre in Lake County.

Seminole County (pop: 370,000; area 350 square miles; administrative capital Sanford)

Orange County (pop. 900,000; area 1,000 square miles; administrative capital Orlando) **www.orangecountyfl.net**

Orange County is located in the centre of the state of Florida, halfway between Jacksonville and Miami. It is well served by major roads. In recent years the population of Orlando has passed the 1 million mark (Orlando extends also into Seminole County). Even so, house buyers can still find a family home for around $150,000. You will also find around ten British and Irish pubs in Orlando, and three more in Winter Park (see www.sunnybrits.com for a full list). I have seen estimates putting the total number of British in and around Orlando in the region of 100,000. For further information see **www.orlandonbritishclub.com**. You can order brochures providing information on living in Orange County, and doing business in Orange County, from **www.orangecountyfl.net**.

Osceola County (pop. 175,000; area 1,500 square miles; administrative capital Kissimmee) **www.osceola.org; www.osceola.com**

The county seat, the city of Kissimmee, is at the far north of the county, and only 18 miles to the south of Orlando. This part of the county is urban, well developed and expanding, and contains most of the county's population. There are a small number of pubs in Kissimmee, including the Fox and Hound Pub at 3514 W. Vine St. To the south and east of Kissimmee the landscape is characterized by ranch lands, prairies, woods and marsh. To the west the county is bordered by the Kissimmee River. The county boasts a large number of creeks (many only partially accessible), and is known for its ideal fishing locations.

Polk County (pop. 500,000; area 2,000 square miles; administrative capital Barlow)

Polk County is situated in the centre of Florida, and is one of the state's largest counties. Whilst the county seat is at Barlow, the largest city is Lakeland, with a population of almost 100,000. The county has over 500 natural freshwater lakes. Besides tourism, agriculture and phosphate mining are important to the local economy

Highlands County (pop. 88,000; area 1,100 square miles; administrative capital Sebring)

Named after its rolling countryside.

Central East Florida ('The Space Coast')

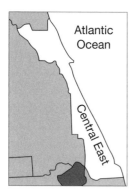

The region boasts over 200 miles of sandy beaches. It is a popular holiday location, and is reputed for its car racing and, of course, for the space launches. Lake Okeechobee is a favourite with anglers. For most of the counties the average winter temperatures are between 17 and 18°C, though Breward is warmer (20) and Volusia rather cooler (15). Average yearly rainfall figures are 48 to 53 inches, save for Breward where the average is as much as 65 inches of rain per year.

The counties

Volusia County (pop. 450,000; area 1,200 square miles; administrative capital Deland) **www.volusia.org**

Volusia, on the Atlantic coast, enjoys 47 miles of truly beautiful Atlantic beaches. Its beach resorts include Daytona Beach, one of Florida's most popular holiday destinations, with its miles of flat white sands stretching out as far as the eye can see, and wide enough to enable the authorities to allow visitors to drive on them. Whilst there is a full range of water sports, the county is best known for the history of car racing on its wide beaches. Ormond Beach is often referred to as the 'Birthplace of Speed'. Daytona International Speedway attracts many visitors for the Daytona 500, a world-class racing event. Disney World and the Kennedy Space Center are about an hour away.

On a quieter note the county is proud of its wildlife reservations, and fishing enthusiasts enjoy spending many hours on the banks of St. John's river. The county's capital is DeLand, with many historic buildings. Information on local history can be found at **www.volusiahistory.com**. Details of the wide range of cultural, sporting and recreational opportunities can be discovered at **www.volusia.com**. The cost of modest-sized family homes in Volusia County starts from under $150,000, cheaper than in the areas further south.

Volusia is a prosperous county with a substantial manufacturing base, and growth in information technology, financial and professional services.

Brevard County (pop. 500,000; area 715 square miles; administrative capital Titusville) **www.brevardcounty.com**; **www.allbrevard.com**

Brevard County, located on Florida's Space Coast, bordering the Atlantic Ocean, boasts stunning white sandy beaches lined by numerous barrier islands. Here you can surf, snorkel, swim, sail, watch the turtles, and fish. Elsewhere you will find numerous parks and golf courses. The Kennedy Space Center, Brevard Zoo and the Brevard Museum of Art and Science are all a must. Disney World is less than an hour away by car.

For information on viewing shuttle launches telephone the Nasa helpline (321) 867 4636. There are numerous places from which to witness a space launch, including the beaches south of Port Canaveral, and along the Indian River. If you want to get really close up, ask about the Launch Viewing Opportunity Ticket by telephoning (321) 449 4444.

The creation of the space agency inevitably prevented other development around the site, and accordingly the surrounding area forms part of a large nature sanctuary.

Okeechobee County (pop. 36,000; area 900 square miles; administrative capital Okeechobee City)

The name of this county, and of the lake from which it takes its name, is of Indian origin and means simply 'large water'. This beautiful lake has also brought death and misfortune to many, primarily after heavy rainfall when its waters have flooded over adjacent land areas. An estimated 1,800 people are thought to have died since settlers first arrived. Today such disasters are no longer repeated, thanks to a complex system of measures to control the movement of water, including the 35-foot-high wall along route 27 from De Belle Glade to Clewiston. Around the lake grow acres and acres of sugar cane that have made Clewiston prosperous. At the extreme north of the lake is the town that shares the lake's name, around which are grown thousands of hectares of vegetables in the drained swamps.

Martin County (pop. 130,000; area 750 square miles; administrative capital Stuart)

Has not grown as rapidly as other counties. The local authorities put an emphasis on protecting the environment. They have imposed a four-storey height limit on buildings, and have made special provision for wetlands and other environmentally sensitive areas. The oldest building in the county is the Gilberts Bar House of Refuge, dating from 1875, and a marine museum and former coast guard station that has been categorized as a National Historic Landmark. A must for visitors, and of substantial educational value, is the Florida Oceanographic Society Coastal Science Center, with its library, nature trails and visitor centre. The Jonathan Dickinson State Park is a 10,000-acre park containing numerous species of plant and wildlife. Activities include hiking, camping, and canoeing on the Loxahatachee River. There is a variety of programmes for children organized via the Parks and Recreation Department during the summer months (see **www.parks.martin.fl.us**).

Indian River County (pop. 120,000; area 620 square miles; administrative capital Vero Beach) **www.ircgov.com/**

Kelly's Irish Bar is at 484B 21 St., Vero Beach.

St. Lucie County (pop. 200,000; area 650 square miles; administrative capital Fort Pierce) **www.stlucieco.gov**; **www.visitstluciefla.com**

The South

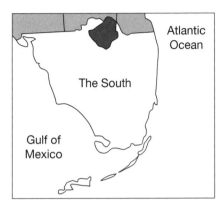

This is the Florida that is most popular with residents of the northern regions of the United States, of Canada and of northern Europe. It is also the Florida that is the first port for many economic immigrants from the Caribbean, central and southern America, making the south a rich cosmopolitan mix. South of Lake Okeechobee, the climate becomes definitely tropical. Whilst the summers may be too hot for some, the winters are wonderful! As you travel south, not only do temperatures rise, but so too does the population density, and the cost of housing. The centre of the peninsula is, of course, home to the Everglades National Park, one of the world's largest sub-tropical reserves. For information generally in relation to the southern half of Florida, visit **www.southflorida.com**.

Southwest Florida

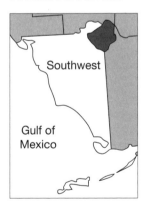

For the most part the coastal areas of this region are far more highly populated than elsewhere in the peninsula, with many permanent residents having moved here from colder climates, and a large number of properties being owned by 'snowbirds' – northerners who come to live in the region during the cold winters of their northern homes. The region is noted for its fashionable resorts, including Naples and Venice. An estimated 10,000 islands line the coast of this region. There is a wide range of leisure pursuits available, including golf.

The average winter temperature in the southwest is around 17°C for all counties, save Collier where the average winter temperature is rather higher (20). Average summer temperatures are around 27–28 throughout the region. Most counties have an average rainfall between 50 and 52 inches a year, though the average is around 58 for the counties of Sarasota and Hardee.

The counties

Hardee County (pop. 27,000; area 640 square miles; administrative capital Wauchula)

An inland, sparsely populated county.

Sarasota County (pop. 330,000; area 725 square miles; administrative capital Sarasota) **www.co.sarasota.fl.us**; **www.exploringsarasota.com/**

The coast of Sarasota is lined by the Gulf Coast Islands. The area has a rich cosmopolitan mix, and is often referred to as 'The Cultural Center of Florida'. This county boasts some first-class museums, as well as art and antique galleries. There is an ample menu of evening entertainment, including ballet, opera, theatre, comedy acts and jazz. In the daytime, activities include fishing, boating, swimming, as well as over 50 quality golf courses. On Anna Maria Island, particularly Holmes Beach and Bradenton Beach, you will find a wide range of water sports, and a vibrant night life. Siesta Key is home to the Crescent Beach, said to rank in the top 10 of the world's beaches.

At Venice, often known by the title of 'The Sharks Tooth Capital of the World', is the longest beach in Sarasota County. Caspersen Beach, on the other hand, is probably the least developed and popular with those wishing to hunt for seashells and pre-historic sharks' teeth.

Not surprisingly, the cost of housing in Sarasota is somewhat higher than most other areas in Florida.

Charlotte County (pop. 145,000; area 860 square miles; administrative capital Punta Gorda) **www.charlottecountyfl.com**

Collier County (pop. 255,000; area 2,300 square miles; administrative capital Naples) **www.co.collier.fl.us**

Collier County is one of the largest counties of Florida. With miles of glorious beaches, you will not find it difficult to understand why this stretch of western Florida is known as the Paradise Coast. Inland, the county is home to prairies and wetlands teeming with wildlife. Attractions include the beaches of Naples (with its immense beach-side homes, and one of the highest-priced property markets in Florida), Marco Island and the Everglades. You will have the opportunity of golf, both saltwater and freshwater fishing, hiking and exploring, as well as more relaxing activities in the spa resorts. For details of the activities available, and in relation to general aspects of living in Collier County, visit the website **www.ParadiseCoast.com**, or call (800) 688 3600. Free visitors' guides are available from the county's Convention and Visitors Bureau office which can be contacted on (239) 403 2384. There are several pubs in Naples (two on 5th Avenue South), and the English Pub, 2408 Linwood (**www.naplesenglishpub.com**).

Hendry County (pop. 37,000; area 1,200 square miles; administrative capital LaBelle) **www.hendryfla.net**

Lee County (pop. 450,000; area 1,200 square miles; administrative capital Fort Myers) **www.lee-county.com**

Tropical, exotic, away from it all, a place out of time. All these descriptions serve to describe Lee County, an environment somewhat quieter and more relaxed than most of southern Florida, with its hundreds of mostly uninhabited barrier islands, and wild unspoilt deserted beaches. Two of the largest barrier islands are Sanibel and Captiva, accessible from the mainland via a 3-mile long causeway. On the former island you will find the Darling Refuge which provides protection for a number of endangered species, including snakes, alligators, turtles and eagles. Property prices have gradually risen over the past decade, though you will receive much more for your money than in affluent Naples to the north. You will almost certainly be able to purchase a modest family home for a little over $150,000. There is a long-established British Club in Fort Myers that meets monthly at O'Sullivan's Pub, Fort Myers. For info call President Nick Gower (239) 945 2043.

Southeast Florida

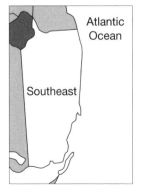

This is the most fashionable region of Florida, popular with the rich and famous. The largest city is Miami, known for its particularly high crime rate, but also for its cultural diversity – it is the home of many Hispanic first- and second-generation immigrants from Haiti, Cuba and Nicaragua. A vast area of the southeast (as well as much of the southwest) forms part of the Everglades National Park, in which there is a wide variety of different forms of landscape, plant and wildlife, including both crocodiles and alligators.

The average winter temperature is around 19–20°C, save for Monroe where the figure reaches 21, and Glades where the average winter temperature is somewhat lower at around 17. The average summer temperature is a fairly constant 28°C throughout the southeast. Average rainfall varies considerably over the region, ranging from 38 inches a year for Monroe to 65 for Broward.

The counties

Glades County (pop. 11,000; area 990 square miles; administrative capital Moore Haven)

An inland rural county bordering on Lake Okeechobee, with by far the smallest population of the counties in the southwest.

Palm Beach County (pop. 1,200,000; area 2,400 square miles; administrative capital West Palm Beach) **www.co.palm-beach.fl.us/**

Palm Beach is one of the most affluent areas in the state of Florida, and the retirement home of many a wealthy American. Otherwise known as the 'Gold Coast', owing to the many treasures recovered from the large number of Spanish galleons that sank along its long coastline. The county's prosperity owes much to the wealth brought by its retired residents and the many tourists who visit each year, but also to healthy construction and agricultural sectors (over 10 per cent of the United States' sugar is produced here), not to mention high-tech industries.

One of Florida's two largest counties, Palm Beach boats a prosperous urban area, wetlands and over 200 square miles of the Everglades within the Loxahatchee National Wildlife Preserve. There is a wide range of third-level educational institutions in Palm Beach County, including Florida Atlantic University (which also has graduate and continuing education programmes), Palm Beach Atlantic University and Northwood University which specializes in business and management. Recreational opportunities abound, not least golf, with more than 150 public and private golf courses across the county. Polo is also played, with a world tournament each year. Other activities include tennis, drag racing, motorcycle racing, boating, in-line skating, shuffleboard, croquet, snorkelling, diving and water skiing.

Palm Beach County also offers a rich variety of cultural attractions with regular events including classical concerts, theatre and ballet. One of the most noted locations is the Raymond F. Kravis Center for the Performing Arts.

There are three pubs in West Palm Beach (O'Shea's and Rooney's both on Clematis St, and the John Bull English Pub, 801 Village Boulevard), and four more in Boca Raton, including the Boca Blarney Stone Pub, 7200 N. Dixie Highway, and the Lion and Eagle at 2410 N. Federal Highway. There is a British Network in Boca Raton for business and professional people to meet up and exchange ideas. It sometimes meets at the Wishing Well Pub on Mizner Boulevard. For further information see the website www.BritishFlorida.com. For lists of cultural groups in Palm Beach, visit the community pages of **www.sun-sentinel.com**.

Property prices in this county are generally high, especially in such areas as West Palm Beach and Jupiter Island, where the word astronomic quickly comes to mind!

Broward County (pop. 1,600,000; area 1,205 square miles; administrative centre Fort Lauderdale) **www.broward.org/**

Property prices in Fort Lauderdale, and indeed in most of Broward County, have risen dramatically over the past decade, making the area one of the most expensive in the south. You are unlikely to find a reasonably sized family home for under $250,000 and will probably have to pay rather more. There are about a dozen British and Irish pubs in Fort Lauderdale (see **www.sunnybrits.com** for a full list), as well as Brady's Irish Pub at 986 State Road 7 in Margate. There is a Fort Lauderdale British Women's Club that meets monthly. Call Norma (954) 563 4061 or Huggie (954) 7648706. The local newspaper is the *Sun-Sentinel* – see its website at **www.sun-sentinel.com**, which includes details of local cultural groups on its community pages. You can obtain further information about the county, and Fort Lauderdale, from the Greater Fort Lauderdale Convention & Visitors Bureau, 100 East Broward Blvd., Suite 200, Fort Lauderdale, FL 33301, tel: (954) 765 4466, **gflcvb@broward.org**.

Dade County (pop. 2,300,000; area 2,400 square miles; administrative capital Miami) **www.miamidade.gov**; **www.miamibound.com**

A large proportion of the county's population reside in Miami, a vibrant city containing many different ethnic influences and inhabitants. The Latin influence is very much present, with thousands of Cubans having settled here from their island home, less than 100 miles from the Florida Keys.

For many foreigners the city of Miami brings to mind crime and violence, thanks in large part to the TV series *Miami Vice*. Between 1992 and 1998, however, the authorities waged a vociferous anti-crime campaign that had a major impact on tourist-related crime. This resulted in a substantial increase in visits by tourists to this colourful city.

The name Miami, which is also the name of the river that flows into the Biscayne Bay, originates from the native-American word for 'sweet water'.

Property prices in the residential areas in Miami are significantly above those in the northern half of the state, and you can expect to pay around $250,000 for a reasonably sized family home. Coconut Grove has become very popular and very expensive. Despite the size of Miami, and the thousands of British living in this busy city, you will only find a couple of pubs (Churchill's Hideaway and Playwright Irish Pub), and following the closure of Hubbard's Cupboard there is no British shop in Miami. There is, however, a British network (see information on the website **www.britishflorida.com** or telephone (305) 371 9340). Not far south of Miami is Coral Gables, a kind of American 'Venice' constructed by George Merrick in the 1920s, which is home to the Crown and Garter public house.

Popular attractions within a short drive from Miami include Lion Country Safari (**www.lioncountrysafari.com**) a drive-through safari featuring thousand of animals roaming free with kennels available for pets; Butterfly World **www.butterflyworld.com**; Native Village Zoo, a zoo and wildlife sanctuary dedicated to 'eco-tourism', where you can experience a wonderful encounter with wildlife; Miami Seaquarium where you can see Lolita, the Killer Whale and TV superstar Flipper, as well as sea lions and dolphins, crocodiles and white-tailed deer; Miami Metrozoo with its lions, tigers and bears and several unusual creatures seldom seen in captivity; the Ancient Spanish Monastery built in Spain in the 12th century, and brought to America by the newspaper magnate William Randolph Hearst; Coral Castle, a walled palace built out of 2 million pounds of coral stone – by one man working alone and who claims to have discovered the secret to how the pyramids were built as he moved enormous stones around the site; Monkey Jungle with monkeys living in a tropical rain forest environment; Parrot Jungle Island www.parrotjungle.com, a world-renowned bird sanctuary featuring entertaining bird shows.

Monroe County (pop. 80,000; area (land only) 1,000 square miles, with over 2,700 square miles of water; administrative capital Key West) **www.co.monroe.fl.us**

Monroe County is very sparsely populated. It embraces much of the Everglades National Park, and over 800 islands, all but about 30 of which are uninhabited. The Florida Keys are a chain of very low-lying islands stretching over 220 miles in a southeasterly direction between the Gulf of Mexico and the Atlantic Ocean, and linked as far as Key West by an amazing highway (Route 1) that includes nearly 20 miles of bridges. These islands are noted for the extreme beauty of their flora and fauna, and the living coral reef. Visitors come here to dive, to fish and to go boating. Whilst Key West is sometimes thought of as the administrative capital and houses nearly a third of the population of Monroe County, these islands are so spread out that in practice there are three separate administrative centres. Not surprisingly, the cost of living in the Florida Keys is high – higher than anywhere else in Florida.

Tourism is the mainstay of the local economy here, although a number of local residents are employed in the fishing industry.

Not surprisingly, housing is expensive in the Keys, and even in the Lower Keys where prices are at their lowest, you will need to spend over $250,000 for a modest family home, with prices over 50 per cent higher in the Upper Keys. You will find a friendly welcome at Finnegan's Wake Irish Pub and Eatery, and Irish Kevin's in Key West.

BUYING IN

To learn all there is to know about the 'best value' homes for sale throughout the 'Sunshine State' talk to the Florida real estate experts & their team from ITV's **'I Want That House'**

Graham Pyle   Allen Jackson

FLORIDA
COUNTRYSIDE

For a free CD-rom Buyers Guide

call

08456 444 747

www.floridacountryside.com

From within the US only call toll free 1-877-298-3931

Orlando $340,000

4 beds * 3 baths * fully fitted kitchen * heated swimming pool * fully furnished
This luxury vacation-home is located some 15 mins drive from the Disney main gates

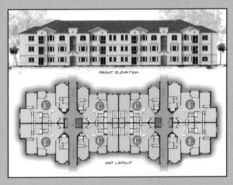

FRONT ELEVATION

UNIT LAYOUT

FLORIDA
COUNTRYSIDE

Orlando from $200,000

Gated resort community of 2, 3, 4 bed condominiums
with clubhouse facilities close to championship golf
courses within 10 mins from Disney

Brits continue to invest
in the "Sunshine State" of Florida!

From the estimated 80 million people that annually visit Florida, a staggering 50 million will travel to Orlando, the "holiday playground of the world". Many folks will end up purchasing property in the "Sunshine State" during their visit and as it is the #1 long-haul tourist destination for UK travellers it is therefore hardly surprising that 50,000 plus homes in Florida are now thought to be British owned.

Most UK buyers will purchase a Florida home primarily for investment and personal holiday use, for property is affordable and yet prices continue to rise. With such an overwhelming volume of visitors, most who will be staying in hotel accommodation there is a strong demand for privately owned accommodation particularly those that are located close to the theme parks and other major attractions.

The opportunity for homeowners to obtain what potentially can be a healthy return is indeed most tempting and yet not every property available for sale will be suitable or indeed capable of satisfying the needs of a typical non-resident buyer.

Like all investment property purchases contemplated within a foreign country it will pay dividends to speak with those who know and this where local knowledge is paramount. Some properties will naturally fair better for investment than others and great care is always necessary to avoid costly mistakes occurring. In Florida the same rule applies, for there are several pitfalls to avoid within the Florida property market, especially if you want to rent out your property during absence.

Unlike their counterparts within the UK, estate agents or realtors as they are called in the US, will have an option to act for either a buyer, seller or they can even decide to remain impartial within a transaction. They do have an obligation to declare their interest from the outset however and a strict body called FREC (Florida real estate commission) governs them.

However should they choose to act for a buyer, the seller still pays the sale fee and this is collected and distributed by the title agency that handle the title deed conveyance and an insurance policy is subsequently issued to the buyer upon closing (completion) warranting the deed.

The US realtor will often be a member of a board, which allows access to the Stateside & National Multi listing system (MLS) and this allows any listed property to be sold by any member realtor regardless of who listed the property for sale.

As such instead of spending time looking for a suitable home to buy, non-residents are best advised to find a suitable real estate firm or realtor to act in their best interests prior to considering any property purchase, just like you would back in the UK when searching for a suitable solicitor representation.

Graham Pyle, a former UK estate agent who has been involved with the "British property buying phenomena" for some 20 years, has gained sufficient valuable knowledge to share his knowledge of the potential pitfalls to avoid with his clients, as well as the many obvious benefits.

Nowadays he conducts information seminars on the subject from his UK Hertfordshire base, where a direct satellite link to his business partner Allen Jackson, the *"Specialist Florida real estate broker"* of ITV's *"I Want That House"* fame, enables his team to keep abreast of the constant changes within the Florida property market. By suitably educating clients, they become qualified to readily strike whenever a suitable property opportunity is available, often without leaving the country!

Having the latest download technology portraying satellite images of the State of Florida, plus access *"on line"* to all listed property for sale, result in many purchases "off plan".

The booming property market in the *"Sunshine State"* means buyers often have to strike from a distance and the high tech information assists such a move greatly.

We asked Graham for some important tips for anyone considering a Florida property purchase.

"In my opinion the most important issue for any non resident considering buying a Florida property is to focus on all elements regarding the possible rental of the soon to be purchased Florida home"

All are best advised to consider the likelihood of rental income ever being required during ownership and even if this is not required from the outset, whether at any time in the future this could change. Most non- resident buyers seek rental income at some point during ownership, for they do not want to leave their US property vacant!

Next is to consider the amount of time will be spent as owner occupiers and how important flexibility of use is.

Lastly assuming rental income is required, is the amount of rental return and possible future capital appreciation

The answers to these questions in most cases normally determine what and where the person should consider buying for the choice is now severely depleted!

Prior to 1990 no real rental restrictions existed for residential property within Florida. Things changed after thousands of "Brits" discovered the merits of a Florida home purchase and many opted to seek rental income in an effort to try and cover the purchase cost!

As a result a couple of counties in Orlando imposed land - zoning ordinances in order to provide some control and similar action was later copied in other places within Florida, for similar problems were encountered when increasing numbers of people discovered other locations, bought property and then let their home to tourists on a "short term" basis.

Today restrictions operate throughout calling for great care to be exercised.

Strict US immigration controls limit the amount of visit time non- residents enjoy without a suitable visa & therefore most non-resident owners seek rental income during their absence.

It is worth remembering that a *"short term rental approval"* does not provide an *"obligation"* to rent out the home it merely provides the approval to let the home on a flexible basis! However when a property is built on land with NO zoning it is possible for a zoning ordinance to be implemented at a later stage!

Bradenton and Clearwater are 2 examples where this has already occurred!

Undoubtedly the best place to obtain a truly profitable return is within the 15-minute catchments of Disney Orlando although caution is required.

Location defined; find yourself a qualified real estate broker specialising in the type of property you hope to find and if holiday rental income is required, find someone in the "short- term investor market" for this would be your best option.

Be sure any brokerage you use in Florida is licensed by FREC (Florida real estate commission) and we recommend that you seek to ensure that no conflicts of interest exist; for example there may be an incentive for the real estate firm to steer you to a specific firm, which is not in your interests. This sometimes occurs when an owner and/or realtor is involved with a single management and/or development firm for it is common to find a buyer in difficulty when this has occurred due to a conflict of interest existing!

It pays to be careful of a glossy brochures portraying *"too good to be true"* rental income proposals!

Ensure that the Florida brokerage is a member of the MLS (multiple listing service) enabling access to the maximum choice of homes for sale, for they have will the authority and access to sell any listed homes for sale!

Recently a change in the property market activity has occurred due to the recent high price increase some 30% plus in 2005 in some cases!

Condominiums with resort facilities are fast becoming attractive propositions for investors for they can attract a similar kind of rental return to a villa and often they will be capable of providing a higher yield / return due to their *"value for money"* pricing and settings often in central locations.

Condos are historically popular with North American buyers and many places such as Miami Fort Lauderdale Sarasota and Naples offer a wide selection of this type of home. It is not uncommon to find investment buyers clambering for new condos developments when *"of plan"* opportunities are first announced. The same pattern is now emerging in Orlando for land values here are soaring, resulting in developers having to increase their land housing density and condo developments do just that.

This is an attractive option for there is an ever- increasing demand for low maintenance homes from overseas homebuyers, most who are keen to find an easy way of increasing their potential financial returns.

Established condos in Orlando can start from as little as $150,000 whereas most new homes now start from around $200,000 and many are just as large as single family home villa. It is after all the number of people that a property sleeps that often determines the obtainable rental sum.

New-detached 3 or 4 -bedroom villas with a private screened pool will start from around $320,000 although there may be some lower priced established resale homes to be found. Of course villa prices just like condos can rise well into the millions of $ it will all depend on the size spec and location what else it has to offer!

Florida Countryside offers a free buyers guide upon request or you can download a pdf version from their website www.floridacountryside.com where you can also find a list of dates for their UK information seminars and exhibitions

The UK office can be reached on **08456 444 747 (local call rate)**

F L O R I D A

C O U N T R Y S I D E

3 Renting a home in Florida

Reasons to rent

Purchasing a property is a serious business. While property prices are generally lower in Florida than in the UK, there are nevertheless substantial costs associated with acquiring property. Choosing the wrong property or the wrong location will be an expensive mistake. Once you have purchased, you may not be able to sell and purchase elsewhere for some considerable time, and when you do there will be significant costs attached. Accordingly, you should give serious consideration to renting a property before you buy. Even if you know well the area in which you intend to purchase, living somewhere is naturally very different from the occasional holiday, particularly if your holidays have all been during certain months of the year. Renting, whether a furnished or unfurnished property, will give you the time to look around, consider your options and decide if the area does indeed fit your requirements after all.

In deciding whether to rent or buy you will need to consider:

▌ whether or not you have sufficient finances to cover the initial outlay of purchasing and can afford the monthly instalments;

▌ the size of the property you require – it is likely that you will be able to afford to rent a larger property than you will be able to buy and, in the short to medium term, this may suit your plans better than buying;

▌ the rental market – in some areas, the rental property market can be very limited, with far greater choice being available to those able to purchase their own home;

▌ whether or not the size of your family is likely to change over the following years;

▌ your job security and the availability of insurance for loss of employment;

▌ your age – it is obviously preferable to purchase prior to age 45 in order to be able to pay off your mortgage before retirement;

■ whether or not your job is likely to require you to move and to what extent your employers will cover relocation costs;

■ the likely rate of growth in the value of property in your chosen location – the value of a flat in the more popular coastal areas in the south of Florida is likely to rise faster than the value of a house in the remoter parts of northern Florida, for example;

■ how much time you have available to carry out your research – the purchase of a property inevitably calls for more expenditure of time than does choosing a property to rent;

■ whether you wish to tie up the capital required for the purchase of your property.

I would strongly recommended that anyone moving to Florida, or even intending to live there for several months of the year, should rent initially, if only for a few months. It enables you to familiarize yourself with the locality and the various amenities (or lack of them). It allows you the opportunity to get to know an area and some of the local population. Far better to read in the local paper about protests about a planned new road or other major development while you are renting, than after you have sunk your hard-earned savings into what turns out to be a living nightmare. It also permits you to search around for an attractively priced property and to take advantage of any bargain that may come onto the market. One disadvantage, especially in the more popular areas, is that prices are constantly rising. If you rent for too long, you may jeopardize your purchasing power.

I would also strongly recommend that you do not enter into a rental agreement before arriving at your destination in Florida. Instead, book two weeks or so in short-term or holiday accommodation. If you are intending to rent for only a year or less, do give consideration to a furnished letting.

Finding a home to rent

There are many different publications and websites where you will find properties advertised for rent, many of them being let by fellow Britons or Canadians who have already purchased a holiday home in Florida. Once in Florida, you will find advertisements in most of the local newspapers, but also via the various ex-patriot British or Canadian websites and associations. Reputable estate agents, however, can often prove very helpful.

One possibility is to enter into a home exchange agreement, whereby for an agreed period of time you live in someone's home in Florida in return for allowing the owner to live in your home. This can be a fairly inexpensive way of living in Florida for a prolonged period, perhaps to facilitate a search for a home to purchase. The risks of a home exchange are obvious and considerable. Further details can be obtained from numerous websites devoted to such exchanges, including **www.homelink.org.uk**.

Visiting the property

Insist on visiting the property at least twice, preferably on different days of the week, at different times and, if possible, in different weather conditions. If you are in search of peace and quiet, watch out for any signs on nearby properties suggesting that building or renovation works are planned.

Protection afforded by Florida law

The rental market is subject to regulation by Florida law, which provides a certain degree of protection to tenants. In general, however, tenants receive less protection than in the UK, and far less than in most other western European countries. The law is less indulgent to tenants who fall into arrears with their rent, or who commit some other breach of their tenancy agreement. Accordingly it is far easier for landlords to evict tenants. Those living in accommodation provided by an employer receive similar protection to other tenants.

At a basic level, landlords are obliged to disclose their name or address, or provide a tenant with the name and address of their agent. They are not entitled to cut off your water, electricity, gas or telephone or to change the locks. Such conduct allows you to bring a claim against the landlord in the Small Claims Court. You are entitled to an injunction to prevent any repetition. The court has the power to order the landlord to pay three months' rent by way of compensation (or your losses if these are greater than three months' rent). The landlord must also pay your legal costs.

Landlords are entitled to enter your home without any permission to deal with an emergency. They are also entitled to access to the premises to make improvements and repairs, to show the property to potential buyers, contractors or potential future tenants, but they must obtain your permission as to the date and time of the visit. They must generally give 12 hours' advance notice for the carrying out of routine repairs. These must be completed between 7.30 am and 8.00 pm.

Note that under Florida law, notices to and from a landlord must be in writing. This applies even if the rental agreement itself was oral.

The rental agreement

Read this carefully! Consider having it checked over by a lawyer. Agreements can be oral, but you should insist on a written contract confirming the tenancy and setting out the terms. The agreement should include the names of the proprietor and the tenant, the date the tenancy commences and its length. It should also give a description of the property, the level of rent, the amount of the deposit and purpose for which the property is being let.

The deposit

A deposit is payable on the signing of most rental agreements. The proprietor may be prepared to give you time to pay this – for example, taking half when you move into the property and half a month later. In any event, ask for a receipt. The deposit is paid as a guarantee of the condition of the property and the other risks taken by the proprietor in letting the property. The amount of the deposit is variable, but is often one month's rent. Under Florida law, a landlord is required to inform you of where any deposit or advance rental payment is being held. If bank interest is being earned on this money, you may be entitled to receive this.

When you come to leave, if the landlord does not intend to retain your deposit, he or she must return it to you within 15 days of your leaving the property. On the other hand, should the landlord wish to hold on to the deposit to cover the costs of alleged damage to the property he or she must notify you of this *in writing* within 30 days of your departure, setting out the alleged damage and how much he or she is retaining for each item damaged. A failure by the landlord to provide you with this notification within the 30-day time limit will generally mean that he or she will be prevented from keeping the deposit.

It will be apparent from the above that it is essential that you must inform your landlord when you will be moving out, and provide him or her with your forwarding address. You should do this by certified letter at least seven days before moving out. A tenant who is moving out at the expiry of a written rental agreement is not required to give this notification.

If the landlord fails to return your deposit, without justification, then you should file a claim in the Small Claims Court. The procedure is fairly straight-forward, and the court clerks will generally provide you with any assistance you require for completing the 'Statement of Claim'. A filing fee is payable, though those on low income may be entitled to have the fee waived.

The length of the tenancy

Where the tenancy is for an agreed period, the proprietor cannot compel a tenant to leave before the end of the agreement except on limited grounds (primarily non-payment of rent and causing damage to the property, but also disturbing neighbours, etc). A landlord is not required to grant a minimum length of tenancy, which can be as short (or as long) as the landlord can persuade a tenant to agree. If no time is agreed between the tenant and the landlord, then the time required for a landlord to bring the agreement to an end depends upon how often a tenant has to pay his or her rent. If rent is paid weekly or monthly then the tenancy is renewed each time a rental payment is made. If a landlord wishes to end the tenancy he or she merely has to give sufficient notice. The notice must be in writing. If rent is paid weekly then the landlord must give at least seven days' notice. If rent is paid monthly he or she must give at least 15 days. In all cases a landlord must obtain a court order before evicting a tenant.

Maintenance of the property

A landlord is responsible for the structure of the building. His or her responsibilities include the roof, exterior walls and foundations, the windows, doors, floors, steps etc and also the plumbing. A landlord cannot get out of these duties, although in the case of a single family dwelling or duplex the landlord's obligations can be altered by agreement in writing. If a landlord fails to honour these obligations you may be entitled to withhold your rent. The tenant must, however, inform the landlord in writing of his or her intention to withhold rent, and must do this at least seven days before the rent is due. This is to give the landlord time to rectify the problem. In addition, for most flats, a landlord is responsible for resolving problems such as the extermination of problems such as rat or cockroach infestations and termites. He or she is also obliged to provide adequate locks and keys, safe common areas, refuse removal, heating during winter months and hot and cold running water. A failure by a landlord to comply with *these* duties does not, however, entitle you to withhold rent, though you do have a right to take court proceedings against the landlord to force him or her to honour his or her obligations and/or for damages.

Tenants are liable for damage caused by their family and guests, save for normal wear and tear. They are responsible for minor running repairs to prevent the property falling into disrepair. The tenants' responsibility covers replacing broken windows, paintwork, bleeding of radiators, replacement of bulbs, fuses and light fittings. They must use electrical appliances, including those relating to plumbing, heating, ventilation and air-conditioning, in a reasonable manner. They must ensure that their family and guests do not cause undue disturbance to the occupants of neighbouring properties.

Both landlord and tenant are obliged to comply with their responsibilities under local building, housing and health codes. These tend to vary from county to county and details can be obtained from the Sanitarian at the County Health Department.

Improvements to the property

The tenant does not need permission to carry out minor works, such as the fitting of a carpet in an unfurnished property. However, he or she should not carry out any substantial work or make holes in walls, for example, without the written consent of the proprietor.

The proprietor's right to carry out works

You are unlikely to be able to object to any necessary work that the proprietor wishes to carry out to maintain or indeed to improve the property. If peace and quiet are important to you (especially if you are at home during working hours), it would be wise to obtain the proprietor's written confirmation that no works of improvement will be carried out during the tenancy, save with your agreement. This should be recorded on the rental contract.

Welcome to
Dream Homes Orlando

Dream Homes Orlando offers a free, friendly and knowledgeable service to all our clients in all aspects of property ownership in Orlando, Florida and the wider USA.

Whatever type of property you are looking for or budget you have, we will try to find the ideal home for you. We are able to offer all new and re-sale properties in Florida and have contacts across the United States to enable you to purchase further a-field, should you wish to do so.

We are experts in the Orlando property market and own our own homes, which we rent out successfully. We have been visiting Florida for over 12 years and are regular visitors to Orlando.

We offer new and re-sale holiday homes and condos for short-term rental within 10 to 15 minutes of Disney World. Our knowledgeable fully qualified Realtor will work with you to select the type of property that will suit your family's needs, in a holiday rental area. He has many years of experience and can help and guide you through the buying process. He will collect you from your rental villa or hotel and give you a guided tour of properties that come within your requirements. He will spend as much or as little time with you as you wish and help you to open a US Bank Account. When you find your Dream Home, he will represent your interests to the buyer. At no time will any pressure be put on you to purchase a property. We believe that it is very important for our clients to buy the home they fall in love with. As a Company we have no targets except your complete satisfaction with your new home and will work with you after your purchase for as long as you want.

We can introduce you to a mortgage provider, who will be able to offer you a wide range of loans to suit your requirements, at a very competitive interest rate. Once you have found your Dream Home, we will advise you on rentals and all the other important things that add up to successful holiday home ownership.

In addition to our expertise with holiday homes, we are also able to offer Buy to Let, long term rental homes, which is very much the same as in the UK. You can purchase a home for rental to a US Citizen; usually rentals are 12 months at a time. You do not need to provide furniture or a swimming pool. This should give you a small income each month, but the real gain is in the increasing value of the home, which you can realise when you sell. The only down side is that you cannot use the home yourself.

For those clients requiring a personal service we offer Custom Homes, which can be Architect designed and built to your specifications on a lot of your choice.

There are many different options for investors who may wish to purchase land for development or Commercial Real Estate, which can be rented for offices and will provide an income.

If you would like to live and work in the United States, we are able to offer advice and help in relocating. We have experts that can help you to find a suitable Business and Home and advise you on all the rules and regulations regarding Visas and permanent residence within the US.

We do hope that we will have the pleasure of helping you find your Dream Home.

Call us today and start making your American Dream come true

Insurance

A tenant should ensure that a policy of insurance is in force from the moment that he or she is in possession of the keys.

Subletting

A tenant cannot sublet an apartment without the prior written consent of the proprietor. Even if as tenant you are given permission to sublet, you remain liable to pay any rent not paid by your sub-tenant.

If you are offered a sub-tenancy, you should ensure that the proprietor's written consent has been obtained or, preferably, enter into an agreement directly with him or her. If you do not, and the proprietor becomes entitled to end the tenancy he or she has granted to your landlord, you may well be left high and dry.

Notice to leave given by the landlord

The main difference between Florida on the one hand, and the UK and other western European countries on the other, is the speed with which the landlord can obtain possession, and the relative lack of indulgence of the courts in relation to a tenant's attempts to pay outstanding rent arrears or remedy other breaches of his or her tenancy agreement.

If the agreement is in writing then a landlord can only obtain possession in accordance with the terms of the lease. If there is no provision governing this in the lease, then the landlord must wait until the lease comes to an end, unless you are in arrears with your rent, or have committed some other breach of the agreement, in which case the landlord is entitled to follow the procedure set out below.

If no time is agreed between the landlord and tenant, then the amount of notice a landlord is required to give a tenant to leave depends upon how often a tenant has to pay his or her rent. If you pay your rent weekly then the landlord must give you at least seven days' notice. If you pay monthly he or she must give you at least 15 days. The notice must be in writing.

The above notice periods apply to cases where a tenant is *not* in any way at fault, but the landlord merely wants possession. If you are in breach of your tenancy agreement these notice periods are reduced further! If you are late in paying your rent a landlord can give you written notice either to pay your rent or move out within three days (weekends and holidays are excluded). If you offer to pay, ensure that you obtain some proof that you made the offer (either written proof, or a witness who saw and heard you make the offer), in case the landlord denies this. If the landlord alleges that you have broken some other term of the agreement then he or she must give you seven days' notice. If the breach is something that you can correct, then you must be given seven days to correct your breach.

Once the landlord has given the requisite written notice, he or she must, of course, still obtain a court order in order to forcibly evict a tenant. After the notice period (ie 3–15 days in the case of an unwritten weekly or monthly tenancy agreement, depending upon the circumstances) then a landlord must issue a claim in the local County Court. The tenant is then served with a Summons and Complaint, either by the Sheriff or some other process server.

The time periods for you to take action are very short, and you should obtain advice immediately. The law allows you five working days (ie not counting Saturdays, Sundays and official holidays) in which to lodge your answer with the Court clerk. You must serve a copy on the landlord or his lawyer. **If you do not file your answer within these five days, a landlord can obtain an order to evict you!**

If you dispute the landlord's claim then you must set out in your answer your grounds for denying that the landlord is entitled to possession of the property, that is, that you are not in arrears; that you offered to pay; that you sent a letter to the landlord at least seven days before the rent was due saying that you were withholding the rent, and that the repairs still had not been carried out; that you did not commit the alleged disturbance or that it was not as serious as alleged by the landlord; that the landlord did not send the requisite written letter of notice etc.

If you are genuinely in arrears of rent then you must pay the amount owing (plus any further rent that has become due) to the court clerk with your answer. If you do not, your landlord will automatically be granted an order for possession. If you accept that you owe rent, but dispute the amount claimed by the landlord, then you must file a 'motion' for the court to determine the amount and attach any documentary evidence supporting your case.

In cases where the landlord does not allege any fault, then provided he or she has given the requisite 7–15 days' notice letter, he or she will definitely obtain possession of the property unless his or her real reason is to punish a tenant for exercising some right (eg the right to withhold rent for repairs, to make a complaint to a local building inspector etc), or the landlord's motivation is to discriminate against a tenant, for example on grounds of race, colour, nationality, sex or disability. Such allegations are clearly serious, and if you make them and fail, the judge might find that you were deliberately playing for time. In that case he or she can order that the tenant pay double rent for the period he or she is in occupation after the end of the notice period.

Before you move in

It is essential that a record of the state of the premises is completed before you move in (see Figure 3.1). This is vital if you wish to reduce the risks of a nasty surprise when you come to leave, such as the proprietor blaming you for damage that was already present before you moved into the property. I recommend that you attend the property before you move in, preferably with the landlord or his or her representative, armed with the checklist supplied at the end of this chapter, and go through this document on site. Check that the cooker and any machines included in the letting are in working order.

I suggest that you use a carbon to make two copies or each make your own copy of the completed document. Ensure that they are identical before both signing them. If only one copy is completed and signed, insist on providing the photocopy yourself. If you give the only copy to the landlord, you may cause yourself considerable problems if he or she loses it or otherwise fails to supply you with your copy.

I also strongly recommend that, on moving in, you take a video of the property, paying attention to any particular defects, and post this to yourself by recorded delivery so that you can prove the date that the video was taken. Do not open it unless some dispute arises at the end of the tenancy, in which case open it in front of some third party, such as an attorney, who can vouch for the fact that the envelope was previously unopened.

Where a property is furnished the agreement should include an itemized inventory listing the contents of the property.

RECORD OF CONDITION OF RENTED PROPERTY

TENANT:

PROPRIETOR:

PROPERTY:

DATE OF MOVING IN:

1 = very good   2 = good   3 = passable   4 = poor

Room	Paintwork, ceiling, window-panes	Floors, doors, windows, blinds	Electricity	Cupboards, storage units	Plumbing, toilet installations	Locks, ironwork
Living-room						
Kitchen						
Bed 1						
Bed 2						
Bed 3						
Toilet						
Bathroom						
Hall/entrance way						
Cellar						
Garage						

Figure 3.1 An example of a form used to record the state of a property before you move in

The first challenge for everyone with an interest in exploring the real estate opportunities in Florida is to find out what services are available in England and who do the best select to look after their interests.

The relationship between such individuals and a British based company offering a comprehensive service (from holiday home purchase to commercial real estate) needs to be as smooth as possible. **Florida Villas, Sales and Rentals Ltd** is the first choice for professional services to British Families interested in Florida. Carol Dudley, the Sales Director has the experience and commitment to meet your highest standards for service and integrity. She is a licensed real estate agent by the State of Florida and has sold and purchased property for several years. She is also s member of F.O.P.D.A.C. - The Federation of Overseas Property Developers Agents and Consultants.

In Florida, the affiliate company based in ChampionsGate, just four miles from the World Drive entrance to Walt Disney World is recognised as a market leader in customer service and satisfaction, The staff in Florida will assist in providing a pleasant and interesting review of all the real estate opportunities available and will guide each client with their interests first and foremost.

Your questions, concerns and interests are of equal importance to both companies and all your needs are co-ordinated from your first contact through your holiday home purchase and long after you are enjoying your investment in Florida.

It is important to know that the company you choose will help you every step of the way, from your first enquiry through to the closing and be there for you afterwards

The service Florida Villas, Sales and Rentals are very pleased to offer includes:

- Personal Inspection Trips scheduled to your convenience
- Sales and purchasing - vacation homes, Condo Hotels, business investments
- Exclusive property opportunities
- In house management
- Arranging mortgages
- Opening bank accounts
- Accountancy & taxes
- Wiring funds
- Rental service
- Owners marketing
- After sales service
- Long term investment

FOPDAC
The Federation of Overseas Property
Developers, Agents and Consultants

- Emigration E2 & L1A visas - these could give you the opportunity to live and work in Florida
- Flight & car hire services
- Furniture packs
- Games rooms

When thinking of a Florida holiday home consider the three values, which are:

- -Personal use and enjoyment
- -Rental income
- -Future appreciation

The different types of investment offered are:-

Vacation Homes

This is for the investor, someone who wants that dream home to be proud of. A home in Florida – The Sunshine State – that they can put their personal touches in for example family photos, choosing the furniture, decor and design your own private pool, adding that little something that says "THIS IS MINE! We have something special to be proud of"

Condo Hotels

Also known as condotels, this is an exciting idea that is sweeping the real-estate industry in vacation destinations that combine vacation-home ownership and real-estate investing – two hot trends. Condo Hotels are always found in prime settings in key holiday-vacation destinations. Orlando Florida is a leading family location in the world and is therefore an excellent opportunity for future growth. Condo Hotels are usually higher-end accommodation offering a resort life in premiere locations.

Commercial Real Estate Investment.

Professional Office Centres are available to be built in high growth areas of central Florida. As residential estates are developed in our market area, a demand for professional service follows and office centres become an attractive investment option.

Commercial Retail Store Centres referred to as 'strip centres are available as buildings in a high selection of locations and consist of six to eighteen stores. The demand for available space is also driven by the large residential development.

For your first step on the road to property in Florida contact Carol Dudley for a brochure and full information pack on 023 8026 6222 or e-mail carol@floridavillassales.co.uk or go to www.floridavillassales.co.uk

When you come to leave

A further record of the condition of the property should be completed and a comparison made with the previous one, to determine the extent of any damage caused during your occupation. I recommend that you make a video of the premises before leaving. In the middle of the recording, video a significant news item on the television or that day's newspaper so you can prove that it was not taken earlier.

Resolving disputes

In the event of a disagreement with the proprietor (for example, he or she is refusing to carry out a landlord's repair, or refusing to repay the deposit) you should seek advice. Obviously, instructing a lawyer can be expensive and may be out of proportion to the financial value of the dispute. There are, however, various agencies that provide free advice, including those that represent tenants' rights. Those on low incomes may be able to obtain free advice from various legal services agencies.

If there is a court case pending, ensure that you keep in contact with the Court clerk to find out the date of the hearing.

Assistance in relation to problems with rental properties can be obtained from the Division of Consumer Services' Consumer Hotline, 1 (800) 435 7352 or 1 (800) 352 9832.

WORLD OF FLORIDA

Yearning for warm sunny cloudless skies, exquisite white sand beaches and some of the finest theme parks and leisure amenities on the planet? You'll find it all in Florida, a place synonymous with fun-filled vacations. The self-proclaimed Sunshine State basks in more than 360 days of glorious sunshine a year. So, whether you're house hunting or holidaying, you'll be blessed by a sun-drenched Floridian climate.

At World of Florida we understand your fondness for the Sunshine State and do everything we can to ensure this affection remains intact. Our service is first class. Our style low-key. Our promises genuine. And our reputation all-important. We enjoy going that extra mile to keep our customers happy and it seems only fitting that dreams come true in place renown for its magic and fairy-dust.

Those planning to snap up a holiday home in Florida will enjoy the support our specialist estate agency, established in the UK for over 13 years. Our portfolio of new and resale homes cover all of Florida's most popular destinations, including Orlando, Citrus Hills, Sarasota, Venice, Englewood and Naples as well as Miami, Fort Lauderdale and West Palm Beach. We only employ Independent Buyers Brokers to ensure totally unbiased advice for customers. There is no hard sell. No pressure. No hoops to jump. We encourage you to ask plenty of questions and buy at your own pace. We've even made the paperwork a breeze.

go see...you'll love it.

World of Florida's full management and rental service is designed to give buyers maximum return on their investment. US or UK Mortgages can be arranged and for a minimum 20% deposit a fully furnished 3 bedroom, 2 bathroom pool home could be yours to move in to - with the added benefit of great rental returns.

World of Florida is ISO 9001 Qualified and a full member of the Federation of Overseas Property Developers and Consultants, combining excellence with peace of mind for sunny days - always.

Sunshine, the star spangled banner and your future is just one simple phone call away.

Call today for a colour brochure and you are already half way across the "Pond".

call: +44 (0)1432 845 645
www.worldofflorida.co.uk

World of Florida, St Ethelbert House, Ryelands Street, Hereford, United Kingdom HR4 0LA
t: +44 (0)1432 845 645 f: +44 (0)1432 845 640 homes@worldofflorida.co.uk **www.worldofflorida.co.uk**

no mistakes...

W O R L D   O F   F L O R I D A

call: +44 (0)1432 845 645

www.worldofflorida.co.uk

Florida has experienced a boom in property sales over the past 18 months. This in part is because of the weak dollar, but increasingly so is due to the value and pleasure attained when buying a home in the 'Sunshine State'

People buy a second home overseas for a variety of reasons. For some it is to use as a permanent home whilst for others as a holiday home with rental potential, or some simply view it as an investment to buy and sell. Florida stands out above any other destination, whether it is the attraction dominated Orlando area about an hour from the Atlantic coast or 2-3 hours from the Gulf coast or indeed the Gulf coast itself, it is exceptional value.

Purchasing a home overseas can seem daunting and stressful. Very often, a clients decision to purchase a home off-plan is based purely on an artistic impression. On returning to the UK they are then reliant on the realtor keeping them updated on every aspect, build time, mortgages, furnishing and management etc. There is all this to worry about plus the extra pressure of it being located 5000 miles away.

Being based in the UK, there are no time differences to worry about. We can be contacted seven days a week and most evenings too. You won't have to wait until Monday afternoon to call long distance, we are only a local call away.

At **Florida-Homes-1st**, we thoroughly enjoy selling homes overseas and firmly believe that buying should be just as enjoyable – an adventure! It should not be a journey into the unknown where you are kept in the dark constantly having to chase people for answers. We are there for you before, during and after your purchase.

We cover every development in the Orlando/Disney area, offering the very latest off-plan products available from Condo's and Townhouses to detached pool villas. Through our MLS links we are able to locate a resale to fit all your requirements from a choice of literally hundreds of homes plus we work to your budget, not ours!

Florida-Homes-1st sell beautiful detached pool villas on the Rotonda at Pt. Charlotte. We are associated with a British company that has been successfully building homes there for the past 14 years. This area, situated between Sarasota and Naples, has rapidly gained popularity due to its location being close to the beach and waterways of the Gulf coast. In an area licensed for short- term rental, they are exceptional value homes.

From our first contact, we determine your requirements as to location and affordable budget, holiday home or investment, and at no time do we exert pressure on clients.

We provide an honest, friendly approach to clients, and treat every enquiry in a professional manner.

We promise never to pass on client's details to a third party.

We offer a 3 nights and 4 days personal inspection tour, completely non-pressured where you will be shown every development, at a pace that suits you.

If you decide to buy you will meet the management company, our mortgage advisors and be taken to a bank to open your US account.

"Are you looking to sell your Florida home?" We have a large data- base of clients, both in the UK and US wanting to buy now. We offer a free appraisal, no sale-no fee, and most important no obligation!

"Your satisfaction is ours."

We look forward to hearing from you.

Tel: 020 8460 9903/020 8464 5991
info@abbeyvillas.com
www.florida-homes-1st.com

Florida 1st
Homes

Villas • Condos • Townhouses
Investment • Holiday homes
Mortgages • Management

Florida-Homes-1st cover every development in the Orlando/Disney area. Close to all the major attractions, offering either off-plan or resale homes.

Prices start from $200,000

Florida Gulf Coast:
Beautiful Pool villas on the Rotonda at Pt. Charlotte.

**Prices start from $224,900 + Lot

Florida-Homes-1st offer a complete & personal service, making buying your home in Florida a stress free, enjoyable experience.

"Are you thinking of selling your Florida home?"

We have a large data base of clients that want to buy NOW.

Call **Florida-Homes-1st** for a friendly & professional service.

100 High Street, Beckenham, Kent BR3 1EB.
info@florida-homes-1st.com
www.florida-homes-1st.com
Tel: 020 8460 9903/020 8464 5991

4 The purchase of your Florida home

The first step: deciding on legal advice

Once you have decided to purchase a property in Florida, you should seriously consider consulting a lawyer before you even start your search. Legal advice should cover the various ways in which you can own your Florida property, the options for mortgage finance and the rules in relation to taxation.

It is also important that the lawyer you instruct should have knowledge of taxation and inheritance law of both Florida *and* your home country, as well as Florida property law. I do not know of any attorneys in Florida that have a sufficient knowledge of English law and procedures to be able to advise you fully. In practice house-buyers from any part of the United Kingdom and from Ireland will need to approach one of the small number of lawyers in their own country that has knowledge of Florida law and procedures. There are, however, several Canadian lawyers resident in Florida, including French-speaking lawyers from Quebec, who specialize in advising their own nationals.

Ensure that you obtain a prior written estimate of their fees, setting out how their charges will be calculated. It is usually a percentage of the property price, subject to a minimum charge (or an hourly rate), though you may find a firm offering a fixed price service irrespective of the value of the property.

Methods of owning property

This is one area where advice is most definitely appropriate and should be obtained fairly early on in the formulation of your plans. There are several options available, each with different financial consequences, including what happens with regard to the passing on of the property in the event of your death and inheritance tax liabilities. The options include ownership in a single name, joint ownership, putting the property in the name of your children (perhaps reserving a right for you and your spouse to continue to live there for life) and purchasing through a trust or limited company. With the latter, when you wish to sell the property, you can simply sell the shares in the company, rather than the property.

Whilst many people opt for joint ownership, in the United States this can take three different forms, *a tenancy by the entirety*, *a joint tenancy* and *a tenancy in common*. The normal presumption in the case of a purchase by a husband and wife is that they hold the property as *tenants by the entirety*, a concept unknown in English law. Here both spouses have a right to the whole or *entire* property. The property cannot be taken from you by your spouse's creditors should he or she become insolvent. This is in contrast to a *joint tenancy*, where a creditor can become entitled to the insolvent partner's share of the property, and in many cases force a sale of the property.

In relation to both a *tenancy by the entirety* and a *joint tenancy*, the survivor becomes solely entitled to the property on the death of the other tenant. In the case of a *tenancy in common*, often used where parties are unrelated, each of the tenants owns a fixed proportion of the property, and on his or her death his or her share of the property will pass in accordance with his or her will (or the laws of intestacy if he or she dies without having made a will).

The practical differences between these three forms of joint tenancy are less in Florida than in other states in that in Florida a person's principal home is protected from most creditors. Your home cannot be taken from you by any creditor, except, that is, by the Internal Revenue Service and your mortgage provider.

An additional option, which you may be offered by a developer, is to buy under a leaseback scheme. Here, the purchaser acquires a legal interest in the property, is generally permitted to occupy it for several weeks a year, and eventually will obtain sole possession of the property. In brief, the purchaser buys the property at a discounted price, but agrees to lease the property back to the owner or a related company for several years, during which he or she is entitled to occupy the property for only a set period each year. After the end of the leaseback he or she is in the same position as someone who has purchased the property in the usual way. This may be a convenient way in which to purchase a retirement home 10 years or so before you come to retire.

Thinking of buying property in Florida?

Buying a home in Florida should be a dream come true. But the legal implications of house-buying in the US are very different from the UK, so it's important to take the best advice as early as possible.

As one of only a few law firms in England and Wales with a partner qualified as both an American Attorney at Law and practising English Solicitor, Bristol-based Bennetts Solicitors specialise in Florida. Our extensive knowledge and experience of this State and overseas property transactions can help you to make the purchase of your dreams become reality, smoothly, quickly and at an affordable price.

For a no obligation conversation, ring us today and ask to speak to Kevin Burke.

Tel: +44 (0) 1934 862786
www.bennettlaw.co.uk

Bennetts
Solicitors & Attorneys
Partnership in Law

Do UK residents buying Florida Property need a lawyer?

If you have decided to buy property in Florida, you have made an easy decision. Many in the UK have made that same decision and look forward to many years of enjoying their holidays in Florida. However, do not assume that because we both speak the same language that the property purchase process is the same. The mechanics of conveyancing in Florida vary drastically from that of the UK. As problems and misunderstandings can and do occur, you should consider instructing a lawyer to help you navigate this foreign purchase process, preferably a lawyer who is qualified in and can advise you on both UK and Florida law. This may be important as what is advantageous in one jurisdiction may not always be so in the other. Your goal should be to get your property with as little complication and risk as possible. Without your own lawyer, who will you rely on to watch out for your interests and protect you from complications and potential pitfalls. In Florida, it is title insurance or closing agents, who may or may not be lawyers, who research the local Florida county court property records and seek to transfer good title to you as the purchaser but you must be aware that they do not represent or advise you. Often in fact they are chosen by and represent the sellers' interests. It is only in having instructed your own lawyer that you have someone to advise you of your legal options, the general tax implications, the various ways to hold title, etc. It is only your lawyer who is qualified to negotiate in your interests with various parties, be there throughout the purchase to address legal needs, to review the draft deed, title insurance commitment and other closing documents before the completion or closing. The work done is further described below:

1. Consideration of How to Hold Title:
It is important in dealing with UK buyers of Florida property to advise them with regard to their particular needs. This starts with examining how to hold title, whether in your own name, with someone else as joint tenants, joint tenants with right of survivorship, tenants in common, or through the use of other entities such as trusts or companies. For example, if you are married, you as UK buyers may want to hold property separately rather than jointly as most Americans do. The reason for this is that there is no US inheritance tax exemption for property transferring to a spouse who is not a US citizen and that any such tax is charged against the full jointly held property rather than against half.

2. Consideration of Tax Implications:
Being for U.S. tax purposes, a Anonresident alien@ you as a UK buyer are not in the same position as a U.S. citizen. Your lawyer can assist you with assessing your greater exposure to various U.S. taxes, consider means of

minimising such exposure and make you aware as to what you are and are not required to pay. It is important to note that a lawyer qualified in both Florida and the UK can inform you as to the general tax implications in both the UK and Florida. The way in which you hold the property can potentially save you thousands of pounds and, as set out above, also can have implications upon estate or inheritance taxes when you come to passing your estate on to a spouse or to children. Advice taken regarding taxes and how best to hold title may require decisions be made and action be taken before you ever sign a purchase agreement.

3. Addressing the Purchase Agreement:

In Florida resales, it is commonly the buyer who provides a purchase agreement to the seller. Often this agreement is the FAR/Bar form issued by the Florida Bar and Florida Association of Realtors or the FAR forms issued by the Florida Association of Realtors. The lawyer often prepares addenda to these standard forms to clarify aspects of the transaction. With new builds, the developers all have their own lawyer-drafted customized agreements which they refer to as standard contracts. There is no standard contract in Florida and it is therefore important that the terms of a particular purchase agreement are explained to you so that you understand the terms of the contract which will be made if the seller subsequently signs the agreement. In some cases, the agreement may be amended to help ensure that the contract is not unfairly balanced in favour of the Seller. One such amendment could be an inspection period as environmental, structural, mechanical, electrical, or other defects which the seller is unaware of or which could be labelled as being visible do not have to be disclosed. The lawyer can assist in drafting a clear contract that gives the buyer what the buyer expects to buy in the transaction.

4. Instruction of professionals:

The lawyer is in a position to identify when a certain type of home inspector, valuer, accountant, or other professional is required and will find and or work with independent persons, retain their services and seek to ensure that your interests are protected. In some instances where you have specific needs your lawyer may refer you to independent particular mortgage brokers or estate agents who past clients had been pleased with.

5. Deadline Follow-up

All contracts for the purchase of real property should include deadlines for such matters as inspections, financing, title insurance, surveys, closing, etc. To avoid breaching the contract, it is important to comply with these deadlines. The lawyer can assist the buyer in meeting contract deadlines not just at the early stages but especially prior to closing.

6. Review Closing Documents and Include Protections.

Title closing agencies are the parties who research title and prepare the closing documents. It is not uncommon for errors of title closing agencies= to be found upon examination of the closing documents by your own lawyer. Sometimes buyers are deeded a property they had not agreed to purchase or the owners' title insurance does not cover the buyers' full purchase price. This can be serious especially where there are defects in title as buyers without representation are often not provided a title commitment before closing. Also to be reviewed is the title insurance on which you are to rely should there later be a title defect normally is not comprehensive and always contains exceptions to coverage which in some instances be removed.

7. Preparation of Wills/Trusts

Your own lawyer can prepare a Florida will which is particularised for the unique needs of UK residents with Florida real estate, and will not affect your UK will. While Florida law generally provides that the Florida courts should accept and attempt to follow foreign wills if valid where they were signed, it is because there may be administrative difficulties in some instances, and on a challenge to a foreign will, that a commission may be required to establish the authenticity of its execution. Where desired, a Florida revocable living trust may be set up so that our clients may avoid probate in Florida with its attendant court and legal fees and administrative delays. This will allow the property to still transfer automatically between spouses without using joint ownership and thereby saving taxes. Whether using a will or revocable trust, as there is no spousal exemption for U.S. inheritance taxes for Anon resident aliens@, married buyers should seek to have a AQDOT@ trust inserted so that U.S. inheritance taxes may be deferred until the earlier of the death of the surviving spouse or sale of the property thereby allowing a credit against UK inheritance taxes on the property.

The benefits of having a lawyer come at a cost: legal fees. Buyers who do not have lawyers do not pay legal fees; at least, not unless or until a breach or defect is discovered. Preventive law is less expensive. Legal fees paid to a buyer's lawyer to advise the buyer before signing a contract to purchase and before closing on the contract are much less than legal fees in litigation. Legal fees in litigation are more expensive because it is fueled by opposing parties with opposing claims and positions. There is no crystal ball to determine in advance whether a particular deal will result in litigation so it is best to hire a lawyer to assist in assessing and minimizing the risks of the purchase transaction to the extent possible. A buyer of Florida real estate, whether it is residential or commercial, should always engage a Florida lawyer to assist in the transaction. Otherwise, there is really no one legally on the buyer's side.

Finding a property and negotiating with the vendor

There is a substantial amount of property available in Florida. This is partly owing to the low population density in northern and central Florida. Taken as a whole, Florida is the size of England, for example, but its population is well under half.

Property is generally priced much lower than in the UK, save in the more exclusive areas of the southern coastal stretches. You should be prepared to negotiate. Vendors in popular areas often put an asking price on their property well above what any local purchaser might contemplate, waiting in the hope of selling to a foreign buyer who doesn't know any better. Always bear in mind that some day, perhaps rather sooner than you might like, you will want to sell this property. You are more likely to be able to dispose of it easily if it is the type of property that would appeal to potential Florida, as well as foreign, buyers. For that reason, if you are buying a family-sized house, you may want to consider not being too far from local schools, even if you do not have children of school age. In the *short* term residential property for owner occupation is unlikely to be a lucrative financial investment. While derelict properties are inexpensive, renovation costs are high and it is important to work out a realistic estimate of the likely total cost of your purchase.

If you are buying to let and/or are keen to maximize your overall gain on your investment and have sufficient means, you should consider purchasing a property in one of the more popular areas. The Sarasota area of the Gulf Coast of Florida, for example, has proved particularly attractive to investors because of the combination of relatively high rises in property prices over the past decade, and the shortage of properties available to rent. The wisest and luckiest investors are achieving returns of almost 10 per cent in terms of rental income, with capital appreciation being an additional 10–15 per cent.

Recent years have seen the appearance of a number of specialist magazines aimed at prospective UK house buyers. The articles in these publications are frequently helpful and informative. They also contain various advertisements by British or Canadian estate agents who have set up agencies in Florida to assist British and Canadian purchasers in their search for a dream home (such as Peter Gold of **www.floridabuyahomeforu.com**; tel: (941) 914 1265). They also contain small advertisements from British and Canadian owners, now wishing to sell their Florida home without incurring an agent's fees.

We had been visiting Florida for the past 20 years staying in hotels, villas and even exchanging our UK home with Floridian homeowners. Our love affair with the State continued and we found ourselves enjoying our time there more and more. We now hardly ever visit the theme parks but just enjoy the weather, its laid back life style, and low cost of living.

Three years ago we decided that if we were to continue visiting we ought to explore the possibility of buying our own home in the sun. We felt that if we could remove the cost of holiday accommodation we might be able to visit more often. We saw the added benefit of leaving belongings behind and at the same time felt that we could have more family holidays together, something we all still enjoyed even though our children were in their late 20's. We just seemed to inherit their friends! It always made for an enjoyable time and perhaps that was another benefit of owning a holiday home. People always wanted to come and stay.

Anyway, after viewing many properties we found ourselves sitting in the hot tub trying to decide whether to buy our dream holiday home. You think of all the advantages and the next minute only the negatives. Your heart says yes and your head says no.

You look for some sort of guidance but in the end you have to make a decision and we decided yes. With hindsight it was the right decision. Of course that does not mean to say things do not and will not go wrong. Like most things in life, you make a decision and only afterwards do you find out the answer as to whether it was the right decision or not. Problems still arise occasionally but we are much better at either preventing them or dealing with them now.

Out of buying our home, we began not only renting our home but in time finding renters for other owners. We then moved into working with Brokers in Florida who we found we could totally trust, formed our own company, **Floridays4U Ltd**. working with them here in the UK, and are even contemplating in time a possible relocation there ourselves.

As is often the case it is what you put into anything that determines whether you succeed or not. If in buying your home in Florida you are going to rely on rentals to help with the running costs our experience is that the most successful owners are those who take responsibility for the majority of rentals themselves. Those generated elsewhere are just an added bonus.

It never ceases to amaze me how trusting so many people become when buying. It's perfectly natural to be tempted to buy from those offering you what appears to be the easiest and most lucrative deal, with little work on your part but guaranteed rental returns making instant profits and surplus money. The reality is not always the case. There are many companies in the industry who offer real good value, service and advice, and of course there are others who will offer you what ever they need to, to get you to buy. What do you actually do if they fail to deliver?

It is a far more sensible approach to learn how to make a success yourself of your investment than rely on others to do so.

Our advice is to do plenty of research, work at your own pace, ask those who have been through the process and question some of the things you may be promised. Find some one you trust and stick with them.

When we are by our pool with a glass of our favourite tipple we think it was worth it.

Memories are forever!

Feliks & Noreen Zakrzewski

Floridays4U Ltd is a family business that helps you find the right property for you - not sell you the wrong one.

- We are not sales or target driven and will not become so.

- We offer help in all aspects of purchasing, a free after sales service and help in your marketing and renting.

- We offer a range of rental properties, so that if you wish, you can try before you buy.

- We are homeowners in Florida ourselves.

- We work with a network of reliable colleagues covering most parts of Florida.

For further information please visit our website or contact Feliks or Noreen Zakrzewski on:

You will also find a selection of such advertisements in the quality UK newspapers, as well as such publications as *The Lady* or even *Exchange & Mart*. The internet is also a convenient and frequently used means of locating properties in Florida (for example via an agency that will find you a real estate agent such as **www.realtylocator.com**) or such sites as **www.orlandosunvillas.com** and **www.formosagardens.us** (specializes in advising on relocation).

Of course there are numerous exhibitions of overseas property in London and Toronto and elsewhere. Here you will be offered subsidized inspection trips. While this may be a convenient way to visit properties, you will only be taken to see a restricted range of properties on the particular agent's books, and often you will be obliged to put up with very 'hard sell'.

If you wish to use estate agents (realtors) you have a choice between instructing a buyer's agent, or one who represent sellers. Obviously an agent who is representing the seller will not have your interests uppermost in his or her mind. If you instruct a buyer's agent you are likely to be shown more properties. The best of them will provide you with an excellent service, locating potential homes, keeping you up to date with the purchasing process, negotiating fiercely on your behalf, and answering your questions promptly. They often provide practical information relating to both the properties and the local area. You should supply the agent with as much detail as possible as to your requirements. As to fees, usually the buyer's agent is paid by the seller's agent splitting the seller's commission. The purchaser therefore pays nothing, save for an administration fee of around $250.

There are also several UK-based estate agents. Generally, the UK agents carry out searches of properties being offered by a large number of Florida agents over a wide area to identify properties that might be of particular interest to prospective UK purchasers. Do not assume that advice and information given to you by those with a financial interest in the sale of the property, whatever their nationality, is accurate or indeed truthful. In rural areas, properties are often not advertised at all but are sold by word of mouth. If you have set your heart on a particular rural area, you should also make enquiries in the local shops or bars.

Many British purchasers prefer to consult a British estate agent resident in Florida. You will find contact details of many such agents from the Florida Association of British Business, tel: (305) 371 9340, website **www.BritishFlorida.com**.

When you do find a property of interest to you, do not sign anything before speaking to your lawyer, who, ideally, you have already instructed prior to carrying out your serious searches for a property. Do not rush in. Speak to your lawyer first.

An oral agreement for the sale of land is not enforceable – the agreement must be in writing. The process starts with you making a written purchase offer. Once you have signed the purchase offer it will normally be provided to the seller by either your realtor or the seller's. If the vendor accepts the offer in the form made, then it becomes a binding contract. The purchase offer will state the sale price, the time for acceptance of the offer, any conditions (for example that the contract is subject to a survey or a mortgage offer), the proposed completion date, the amount of the deposit, provision as to how taxes and utility bills are to be divided between them, and provide the purchaser with a final opportunity to walk through the property to satisfy himself or herself that its condition has not changed since the contract was agreed. The offer should be accompanied by the payment of the earnest money (deposit) to an attorney or realtor. If the seller signs that he or she accepts the offer then there is then a binding contract between the parties. If the seller is unhappy about one or more terms of the offer, then he or she indicates this by a counter offer. The purchaser can then either accept this counter offer as it is, or make a counter offer in response. This process continues if necessary, until the parties are agreed on all the terms of the agreement between them.

Once you have made an offer, or a counter offer, you cannot normally withdraw your offer after it has been accepted – though you can do so before acceptance.

A deposit is often referred to as 'earnest' money, or 'putting money into escrow'. A buyer who fails to complete loses his deposit. A seller who is unwilling to complete can be sued for damages, and indeed the purchaser can obtain an order for 'specific performance' of the contract, that is, a court order that the seller proceeds to complete the sale.

As to contents, everything that is permanently fixed to the property is included unless stated otherwise.

Purchasing at auction or following a repossession

As elsewhere, the best-value properties are often those sold at auction by banks and other mortgage providers that have repossessed, or by other creditors seeking to recover outstanding debts, or where there is a dispute as to inheritance, or where the owner has died without heirs and the property needs to be sold. Auctions offer an opportunity to purchase property at sometimes a mere fraction of its market value.

For details of properties available for sale following default in mortgage payments by their owners ('foreclosures'), see **www.hudbox.com**. You can search Florida county by county. It is possible to purchase a foreclosure property with no down payment.

It is essential to inspect the property prior to bidding or, alternatively, arrange for a local estate agent (for a modest fee) to visit the property and provide you with a description and some photographs. Purchasing at auction can become expensive if you have to make several bid attempts before you are successful, especially if you obtain a report from a surveyor or other expert on each occasion.

Viewing the property

It is essential that you view the property several times, including in good and bad weather, and during the hours of darkness. Take care to listen to what noise is likely to affect you. Approach the property from different routes and consider how visitors might approach it. You might not appreciate them remembering that to reach you they have to turn left past the sewage works, continue on past the funeral directors or climb the hill past the refuse dump. You should not be deterred from returning to the property before deciding whether or not to proceed. If possible, try to ascertain why the owners wish to sell and how long (and it may be a question of years, rather than months) the property has been on the market.

Consider the property's location in relation to access to public transport and proximity to shops – chemists and so on. Look carefully not only at the building, but also at the garden and the neighbouring properties. Are the boundaries clearly marked? Is there any reason to suspect that other people have a right of way over the property? What about that well-worn path running through part of the property? If there is some other feature of the property that concerns you, speak to the agent and vendor, then raise it with your lawyer. Check also that the light switches work, that there is hot and cold running water and that the toilet bowls are not cracked.

Buying a home in Florida through Luxury Villas Worldwide (LVW) is simple and straightforward with our guidance.

LVW have built up relationships with professionals in Florida to ensure that you get the best advice and service possible. These professionals include Realtors (estate agents), Mortgage Advisors, Accountants, Management Companies and Furniture suppliers.

Why buy a home in Florida? There are typically three reasons: buying for use as a family vacation home; as an investment, using it for holiday lets to generate income while the capital appreciates; or as a combination of these two reasons. Whatever your reason, LVW is there to make the experience an enjoyable one without any of the potential pitfalls associated with buying abroad.

When deciding what property and where to buy, the reason for your purchase will be a defining factor. Currently, the most popular rental area and one of the fastest capital appreciating areas is around Disney World. For lovers of the sea, the Gulf Coast offers some beautiful locations.

To assist you in choosing the right property, LVW will provide brochures for both new and resale properties that meet your buying criteria so you are able to draw up a short list before your visit to Florida.

When you visit Florida, we will arrange for a Realtor to meet you and personally escort you round the developments and properties that meet your buying criteria. LVW will have briefed the Realtor to ensure that your time is used productively. Using a Realtor does not cost you anything; the builder in the case of new developments and the seller in the case of resales pay all commissions.

If you require a mortgage, we will arrange for a Mortgage Advisor to meet you at your convenience to discuss the types of loans available, lending criteria and repayment options. Loans up to 80% of the value of the property are available with either interest only or repayment terms offered.

During your stay in Florida you will need to set up a Bank Account. Take your passport and proof of your address to the Bank. An opening deposit of $100 is usually required.

If you purchase a property, we will arrange for an Accountant who is an expert in preparing accounts for owners living abroad to explain what records you must keep and what expenses are tax deductible.

If you choose to buy a new property, this will almost always have to be 'off plan' with a wait of six months or more before completion. However, LVW is sometimes able to offer new properties that are almost completed. Many builders include a standard furniture package in the purchase price. These packages can be upgraded in part or whole depending on your budget. If a furniture package is not included, LVW will introduce you to furniture companies that specialise in complete home furnishing packages.

LVW have an association with a Management Company that will look after your property ensuring that it is maintained to the highest standard.

Having chosen your property, you will have to transfer money to Florida to complete the purchase. LVW is able to recommend a company that will handle all your money transfers. On submission of a simple application form your account will be set up the same day.

In summary, LVW has everything in place to ensure that your purchase of a property in Florida is a pleasant, problem free experience supported by experts from all the professions you need to deal with.

Please contact us for further information and allow us to arrange an inspection visit to enable you to find your dream home in Florida.

Whether you are buying an established property, a new one from a developer or purchasing a building plot, you should pay particular attention to the terrain. Attempt to ascertain whether the land is likely to flood. A stream or river may be picturesque when you visit, but may overflow its banks during heavy rain, making your garden unusable even if your house remains untouched. Fortunately, some areas that are prone to dampness and flooding are easily identified by their names. When considering buying, ascertain the meaning of the name of the road or area in case it has a negative meaning.

Whether you are buying property or land, a surveyor can advise you whether the land was or is suitable to build on, especially if he or she is familiar with the locality. Be alert also to the possibility that the land has been used as a dumping ground for refuse or chemical waste – if you are being offered what seems like a bargain, this may be the explanation.

It is wise to visit the local county planning offices to ascertain what improvements are planned in the locality, including any airports, motorways and railway lines. Ask what planning permissions, if any, have been granted for neighbouring properties. Check whether or not the area is subject to flooding.

Surveyor's report

Always consider obtaining a home inspection or surveyor's report. A structural survey has two very important advantages. First, it prevents you from purchasing a property that is structurally unsound, perhaps dangerous, expensive to restore and perhaps difficult to dispose of. Fresh paintwork may be hiding a serious structural problem that is not evident to you. A watermark may have been caused by a one-off incident, or might be an indication of a continuing problem. The report should identify any woodworm and any movement in the property (which may have caused extensive damage to underground drainage channels or undermined the stability of the property). Second, a good report, even a basic one, should identify any non-structural defects – often minor, sometimes more significant. These may not deter you from your intended purchase, but may give you ammunition to negotiate on the purchase price. Ensure that a written report is provided and make it clear what is to be covered – that is, structural condition of roof, walls, foundations, all woodwork, drains' connections with mains or the septic tank, plumbing, electrical and heating installations.

Everyone dreams of "Having it All"!

Just imagine relaxing by your private pool in Florida's warm, sunny tropical climate, your family laughing and splashing in the pool, your wife lounging in the sun next to you.

Everyone's happy as they think about their upcoming trip to the major theme parks: Disney, Universal Studios, Seaworld. You think about breaking 70 in your golf game at the lush, green course nearby.

Sound Expensive? What if we told you that you could make this dream come true AND make money at the same time!

It's true. Classic Florida Realty, Inc. has been making dreams like this come true for years. They specialize in helping folks invest in Florida vacation villas. You can own your own vacation home, take a holiday anytime you'd like, earn rental income while your not there and build equity in the profitable Florida real estate market.

The conglomerate of Classic companies offers all the services you'll need to ensure a smooth transaction. From immigration and visas, to mortgages, currency exchange, home decor, property management and vacation villa rentals, there's a Classic company to guide you every step of the way.

It's a well-known fact: Florida is fast becoming the number one travel destination in the world. After all, Florida boasts spectacular weather year round and offers almost every type of entertainment and recreational activity under the sun. No other place in the world offers the attraction of the major theme parks, championship golf courses, together with miles and miles of beautiful white sand beaches.

Florida's visitors are fast realizing the benefits of staying in a holiday home instead of a hotel. Vacation homes provide the perfect environment for families with spacious living areas, choice of bedrooms and private swimming pools. Away from the hustle and bustle of the tourist areas, but close to major attractions, and conveniences, the vacation villa offers the best of both worlds.

Families like the ability to eat a home-cooked meal any time they want, instead of eating every meal out. They like the privacy that a vacation home offers. Once a family enjoys the comfort and luxury of renting a holiday home, and realizes the exceptional value it provides, very few will go back to staying in a hotel.

Classic Florida Realty can guide you in choosing the right property for your investment needs. As licensed brokers, they represent some of the finest builders and developers in Florida. All of the Classic communities are near world class golf courses, tennis facilities and minutes away from the attractions, entertainment and shopping.

Classic Florida Mortgages funds more than 50 million dollars each year in new business for second home investments around the world. The company offers a complete range of loan products including:

- Fixed rate
- Adjustable rate
- Low Documentation
- Non Status and Interest Only.

Classic Property Management fully appreciates all the concerns of absentee owners and provides complete turnkey, reliable and worry free property management services to ensure your investment is safe and well maintained.

Classic Holiday Villas, the Rental division of Classic, makes renting your home easy! Their sophisticated online reservation system allows travelers to view available vacation homes, take virtual tours, and book the home in real-time. Classic also offers an optional marketing program that includes your very own website, complimented with internet and traditional marketing to ensure your success in the vacation home industry,

Let Classic show you how to make your dream become reality. Call them today to arrange for a low-cost inspection visit. They will fly you to Florida so that you can tour first hand the beautiful homes and communities that are available. A representative will meet you at the airport, escort you to your accommodations and remain on hand throughout your entire visit to answer any questions you may have.

www.classicfloridarealty.com

Classic Florida Realty, Inc.	Classic Florida Realty UK
Classic Florida Realty USA	23 Castalia Square
215 Celebration Place	Docklands
Suite 330	London E14 3NG
Celebration, Florida 34747	
Tel: 800-438-2215	Tel: 0-800-298-9082
Fax: 321-559-1289	Fax: 0-207-987-0239

"Having it All" doesn't get any easier. Give Classic a call or go online to tour some of their property or developments today!

Wishing You Were Here?

DESTINATION: *Florida*

We Make It E-A-S-Y!

Let us show you how easy it is to own your own Holiday Home in beautiful, sunny Florida. Earn rental income while you build equity in Florida Real Estate. From home sales, to mortgages, property management and vacation home rentals, Classic Florida Realty has the expertise to take care of it all!

Call us today for your FREE guide to overseas property investments!

0800 298 9082 (UK)
800 438-2215 (US)

Or search our Extensive Inventory of Holiday Homes online at: www.ClassicFloridaRealty.com/Guide

Your Best Investment Under the Sun!

www.ClassicFloridaRealty.com

In an ideal world you should be present when the inspection is carried out. This enables you to easily raise matters that concerned you. You are also likely to learn more about the property from oral comments made by the inspector that he or she might not include in his or her report.

In addition, in Florida, you should seriously consider having the property inspected for termites.

The cost of a report varies from county to county and according to the value, size, age and other characteristics of the property. You can find contact details for home inspectors throughout Florida from the Florida Association of Building Inspectors (FABI), P.O. Box 149202, Orlando, FL 32814–9202, tel: 1–800–544–3224, e-mail info@fabi.org, or from the American Society of Home Inspection. The FABI is a professional society that operates its own professional code of ethics and produces guidelines to its members for inspections. Its members are independent professionals with a variety of qualifications and experience within the construction industry. It is one of the leading authorities on home inspections. Most house buyers contact the home inspector once they have made an offer on a property, but before signing the contract. You can, however, request a clause in the contract to the effect that the contract is subject to a satisfactory inspection report and obtain the report after signing the contract.

What your lawyer should do

Apart from advising you on the terms of your offer to purchase, and any counter offers, your lawyer should also undertake certain enquiries before you close your purchase:

1. Establish that the vendor has good title to the property. Is the person seeking to sell the property to you the true and complete owner of the property?
2. Carry out a search at the local town planning department to ascertain whether there are any significant new developments in the pipeline that might affect your property.
3. F you are purchasing an apartment or a property in a development, obtain proof of payment of charges levied by the body responsible for managing the development, in particular the common parts), and inspect the rules governing the development, and the minutes of its last meeting. For further details see Chapter 7. Ask your lawyer to ascertain whether there are any items of major expenditure

planned for the foreseeable future. If you have a pet you will also need to know whether pets are permitted.

4. For recently built properties, advise you on the terms of the builder's structural guarantee.

You will need to provide your attorney (or other closing agent) with sufficient funds to pay the purchase price, taxes and other expenses in time for closing (completion). The attorney will be responsible for paying the appropriate sums to the vendor, realty agent etc. Usually he will pay the escrow charges. Remember that in the case of sales by non-residents, the purchaser is obliged to pay 30 per cent of the purchase price to the tax authorities, as security against the vendor's tax liabilities arising from the sale.

The costs of purchasing a property

It is difficult to give a precise estimate of the total costs and taxes involved in a transaction, They include the home inspector's report (around $400), the costs of any other inspections (eg for termites, around $50), a land survey, lawyers' fees, a title search, title insurance (depends on the value of the property), transfer and registration fees. Who pays for these costs is partly a matter of local practice, and partly a question of negotiation between vendor and purchaser. The total fees and charges, including the mortgage arrangement fee, will generally level out at between 4 and 7 per cent of the purchase price

Registration of your purchase

After your purchase is completed ('closed'), the transfer of the property into your name will be registered with the local property records office. You may wish to pay a visit to the office about two or three weeks after completion to verify that the transfer has been recorded.

Insurance

You should consider taking out title insurance. This protects you if the title to the property should prove to be defective. When a property is sold or transferred a title search and examination of public records will reveal most defects in the right of the vendor to sell the property, for example any charges on the property, or joint ownership with someone else. Occasionally, however, there are problems with a title that are not apparent from such a search, often as a result of some fraud or mistake in the past, or present. Title insurance protects you in relation to any claim that your title is defective. You pay a one-off premium which provides you with continuing cover.

You also need to have home insurance cover in place. Ensure that you have sufficient cover. If you under-insure you will not be able to claim your full loss. Public liability insurance is cheap and, accordingly, a high level of cover is worthwhile. When you need to claim, ensure that you do so within the strict time limits and by recorded delivery. If you intend to occupy the property for only short periods or to let it out, you should inform your insurers. Lastly, you should take out flood insurance if you are in a high-risk flood area. This cover is provided by the federal government (see Chapter 8).

FLORIDA MORTGAGE PARTNERS, INC

- FINANCING UK FLORIDA SINCE 1989
- 20% DEPOSITS, NO VERIFICATION OF INCOME
- INTEREST ONLY AND CAPITAL REPAYMENT
- NO OUT OF POCKET EXPENSES FOR RE-MORTGAGES OR EQUITY RELEASE
- WE SHOP DOZENS OF LENDERS SO YOU DON'T HAVE TO!
- FREE PRE-APPROVALS WITHIN 48 HOURS
- PRE-CONSTRUCTION AND LOT LOANS. ALSO AVAILABLE
- STERLING MORTGAGES
- CONDO CONVERSIONS AND CONDO HOTEL LOANS AVAILABLE

SEAN DEPASQUALE

WWW.FLORIDAMORTGAGEPARTNERS.COM

TEL: 001-407-999-0060x101 OFFICE

E-MAIL: SEAN@FLORIDAMORTGAGEPARTNERS.COM

MEMBERS: BRITISH AMERICAN CHAMBER OF COMMERCE AND INTERNATIONAL REAL ESTATE COUNCIL

FEATURED MORTGAGE BROKER ITV "I WANT THAT HOUSE"

Sean Depasquale is the owner of 'Florida Mortgage Partners, Inc.' in Orlando, Florida. FMP is the industry leader in clients from abroad purchasing vacation or buy to let properties. FMP specializes in Vacation, BUY to LET, and re-mortgage of home loans in the state of Florida. FMP has been the industry leader in foreign national loans since 1995. FMP is a fully licensed Correspondent lender and a member of the International Real Estate Council and the British American Chamber of Commerce. FMP has the best reputation in the market for providing high quality, low cost mortgages for our clients. Nobody in the market has as many loan options catered for the Foreign National market as FMP. Florida Mortgage Partners is also the featured lender of Merrick Television ITV *I Want That House*. FMP has over 17 different lenders to choose from so you are assured you are getting the best rates and terms available in the market. They offer pre construction loans, lot loans, Sterling mortgages, self-certification loans up to 80%, loans with NO redemption penalties and more! FMP will have a decision in principle on your loan within 48 hours at no charge. FMP has continuously led the market in offering the best options available for foreign investors. FMP's client base ranges from professional football players and coaches to self-employed business owners. FMP has a 97% approval rate for their clients purchasing in Florida.

Let **Florida Mortgage Partners, Inc.** assist you in the purchase of your Florida Vacation/Assessment home, as you will NOT be disappointed.

Contact: **Sean Depasquale**
Florida Mortgage Partners, Inc.
301 S. Orlando Ave.
Winter Park, FL, 32789
Office: **001-407-999-0060x101**
Fax: **001-407-999-4881**
Mobile: **001-407-620-9898**
Email: **Sean@floridamortgagepartners.com**

5 Financing the purchase of your Florida home

Raising funds on your home property

One option is to raise the finance in your home country by using a property in the UK or Canada as security. The cheapest option may be to ask your existing mortgage lender if it would increase the mortgage facility, thereby avoiding legal fees, land registry fees and even an arrangement fee. You could also take the opportunity of considering re-mortgaging your existing property – you may succeed in reducing your existing repayments to offset partly the costs of financing your Florida property. Using your UK property enables you to take out a PEP mortgage, a pension mortgage or an interest-only mortgage, whereas in the United States you will generally have to take out a repayment mortgage.

The main drawback of borrowing in the UK is that interest rates have in recent years been high compared to the United States, though it is often difficult to compare rates easily between the two countries as they are calculated differently, and the only way is to make a comparison of the amounts of the monthly payments, and the total repayable over the term of the loan. A second disadvantage of a UK loan is that you will almost certainly not be able to set off mortgage interest against rental income for income tax purposes. On the other hand, if you are paying your repayments from funds in the UK, your repayments will not increase if the value of sterling falls.

US mortgages

Taking out a mortgage is a serious and long-term commitment. For this reason, many foreign residents who take out a mortgage in the United

States still prefer to deal with institutions from their home country, There are several British or Canadian banking institutions that provide such a service.

Before deciding on a mortgage lender, you should shop around the main institutions to consider the variations and any special promotions that they may be running. There are a number of mortgage search companies, including over the internet, that will advise on the best offers available. Ensure that you fully understand the policies on offer. Most mortgages available in the United States are some form of repayment mortgage, with fixed or adjustable rate mortgages (ARMs), and many (though not all) impose penalties for early repayment. Taking independent advice may well save you substantial financial loss, not to mention anxiety and heartache. It is important, also, that you only borrow money from an established and prosperous mortgage provider. If your mortgage provider were to become insolvent you could find that the balance on your mortgage could become immediately payable in full to satisfy debts owed to the provider's creditors.

There are now many loan programmes that require only a 5 per cent down payment or less, although if your are putting forward less than 20 per cent of the purchase price mortgage providers generally require a mortgage guarantee from a third party, such as the Federal Housing Administration (FHA) or a private mortgage insurer (PMI), and obviously there is an additional cost to the purchaser.

There are also a number of mortgage providers that allow purchasers to buy homes with no down payments, and several new mortgage programmes that also cover purchase costs. Non-residents, however, with no US credit history, are generally restricted to 70 per cent or less of the value of the property. Obviously the higher the loan, the greater the monthly mortgage payments, and accordingly most purchasers prefer to make some down payment. In a buyer's market it may in any event be possible to negotiate a purchase in which the vendor pays some or all of the costs of your purchase.

Whichever bank or other financial institution you approach, it will need to check your financial standing and will require details of residence status, employment position, income and tax status. If you are self-employed, you will be asked for your accounts and tax liabilities, often over the preceding three years. Arrangement fees vary, it is worth shopping around.

AS GEORGE BERNARD SHAW PUT IT SO WELL: "England and America are two countries separated by a common language." Nowhere is this more true than for UK residents buying villas and other investment properties in Florida, where surveys are 'appraisals', completions are 'closings' and no one is quite sure what an 'escrow' is! It is important, therefore, that British property buyers in Florida not only understand 'both languages' but also keep abreast of the very different buying and selling procedures in both countries. Keeping up-to-date with new ways to find, evaluate, purchase and finance Florida property is an absolute cornerstone of successful property investing in the 'Sunshine State.'

It's important that UK property investors secure the assistance of companies or individuals expert in trans-Atlantic real estate and finance practices. Protected with this expertise UK purchasers will minimise the risks and maximise the personal and financial returns on their investment in Florida property. And these returns can be significant indeed. As the *Central Florida Business Journal* magazine announced this year: "Florida's median existing-home price rises 70 per cent in five years."

Single-family villas with their own private pools are still enormously popular with British investors but escalating land prices, for example, are driving the estates further and further away from Disney in Central Florida.

Enter the "Condo-Hotel"…

Paradoxically, Condo-Hotels (Condominium-Hotels) are the newest 'old' real estate phenomenon in the steaming Florida real estate market – and one which is proving to be of great interest to many UK property investors.

Years ago only celebrities and the very wealthy could afford to live in luxury hotels. Those lucky few did so to enjoy all of the amenities and services that only a fully-staffed hotel could provide. All of that is changing in Florida, particularly in certain popular resort areas such as Orlando and Miami. Now you can purchase your very own hotel suite (that is, a "condominium apartment") at a price affordable to most UK property investors.

Lee Weaver, Director of Operations for The British Homes Group, one of Florida's leading estate agencies (called "Realtors" in the US) and multi-currency mortgage companies, notes "condo-hotels represent a new level of convenience, security, social interaction, service, investment potential and affordability for our UK clients." Also, because of their proximity to Disney and their nightly "rent-ability", the condo-hotel really opens up the short-term rental market to the more than 60 million American vacationers who visit Orlando each year – a potential renter pool unmatched in any other property investment market in the world.

Two new condo-hotels that the British Homes Group is offering to its UK clients are the *Lake Buena Vista Resort and Spa* and *WorldQuest Resort*. The first two phases of both properties were quickly sold-out, mostly to UK buyers. Well-known hotel chains (like Hilton, Gaylord and Remington) are managing the projects which dramatically increases rental prospects. Both new holiday communities are virtually on Disney's doorstep. The British Homes Group is now offering Phase III in both communities and is accepting reservation deposits from new purchasers.

High quality furnishings, fitness centers, clubhouses, 24/7 security, balconies (many with views of the nightly firework displays at Disney), entertainment centres, extensive rental programmes, all for off-plan prices starting at less than 200,000 GB pounds, are just a few reasons why these new condo-hotels, in the heart of the Orlando "Attractions Area", are proving so appealing to short-term renters and UK investors alike.

Why use a "One-Stop" Shop"?
Simply for convenience and cost saving.

Over the past five years the British Homes Group, British staffed, Orlando based, and a member of the Orlando British-American Chamber of Commerce, has grown to become "the United Kingdom's favourite one-stop shop for UK property owners in Florida". The convenience of a "one-stop" shop, for example, means that UK residents can, through one estate agency (unlike in the UK) find, finance, rent, and have access to, all the components needed for villa ownership in Florida.

Both UK and US currency mortgages are available through the British Homes Group but one British Sterling mortgage programme that has proven extremely popular with British real estate investors in Florida is British Mortgages Abroad. British Mortgages Abroad was developed in collaboration with Abbey National and is now offered by the UK subsidiary of GE through British Home Loans in Orlando.

"The British Mortgages Abroad programme" explains Lee, "was developed *specifically* for UK property buyers in Florida. It offers UK investors British currency home loans, secured on the Florida property rather than their UK home, and thereby protects borrowers from any monthly payment currency exchange risk without encumbering their primary home in the UK". Additionally, this innovative pound mortgage allows UK borrowers to take up to six "payment holidays" in any one year, thus giving a high repayment flexibility reflecting the seasonality of the Florida tourism and rental property market – UK investors can now make additional capital repayments in high rental seasons and, if necessary, delay monthly payments in low season – thus eliminating much of the traditional risks of investment properties abroad. An added bonus of a British currency mortgage, if properly structured, is that interest payments may also be deducted from rental income to help minimize or eliminate entirely any US tax liabilities.

British Home Loans also offers a wide selection of fixed and adjustable rate US currency mortgages. "There's nothing wrong with a US mortgage", Weaver notes, "as long as you live in the US and are paid in dollars. But if you live in the UK and are paid in pounds trying to stay on top of a US dollar mortgage can be a real pain!"

To make initial enquiries easy the British Homes Group has set up a UK to USA freephone number – **0800 096 5989** and have a web-site with more information, **www.BritishHomesGroup.com** or, when in Orlando call the company's local office in Kissimmee – **407-396-9914**.

The amount that you can borrow is calculated in a different way from in the UK. In brief, you will be limited to a loan with monthly repayments that do not exceed 30–40 per cent of your net disposable monthly income, that is, your net monthly income after deduction of tax, national insurance and such commitments as mortgage payments on other properties, loan repayments and maintenance payments.

For those purchasing a property in joint names their net disposable incomes can be added together in calculating the total mortgage capacity. If you are buying a property to let, then the rental income can be taken into account, providing the property has a history of producing a rental income. The same applies to leaseback properties. If the property is clearly an investment property, then the lender may insist on applying different commercial criteria under which the mortgage repayments should not normally exceed 80 per cent of the rental income.

If you have been resident in Florida for some time and are purchasing with the aid of a US mortgage, you should ensure that you have a good credit record. This is especially important for those wishing to buy with a zero or small down payment. In practice this means that for at least a year up to your purchase you must ensure that you pay all your credit card bills, rental payments and any other debt repayments in full as and when they fall due. You should also resist the temptation to spend heavily on credit in the run-up to buying your home, or during the purchasing procedure. Even if you have received a 'pre-approval', your mortgage offer will be subject to a final assessment of your financial position. Don't go on a spending spree using credit if you are thinking about buying a home, or are in the process of buying a new home. A further $200 on your debt repayments per month could reduce your mortgage capacity by $20,000. Wait until the purchase of your home has gone through.

If you do not have a sufficient credit history, consider taking out a department store credit card, and a small bank loan over a short term. Ensure that you make payments for both on time. You may be able to obtain a loan without a good credit history. However, you will have to pay an interest premium (sometimes called a 'nonconforming mortgage'), so you might be better to delay your purchase whilst you build up your credit history.

Lenders will generally give prospective purchasers confirmation of their mortgage eligibility ('pre-qualify'), including over the telephone. In reality this is no more than an estimate of your mortgage potential based on the information that you have given them. Most lenders, however, are happy to offer a 'pre-approval', that is, they have considered your application, carried out a credit report and satisfied themselves as to your financial position. This enables you to be certain about the maximum mortgage that you can obtain. Furthermore, the seller will know that you are a serious purchaser and will be more prepared to negotiate knowing that you can honour any agreement.

You should also look out for first-time buyer programmes. The term 'first-time buyer' seldom means someone who has never purchased a property before, and often covers all those who have not purchased within the last three years. These programmes are often backed with public money and enable purchasers to buy with reduced down payments and at subsidized interest rates.

Obtaining your mortgage from a developer

If you are buying a property from a developer, you may find its terms for a loan more attractive than those of a bank mortgage. Do take legal advice before committing yourself, however. A particular point to watch out for is the consequences of late payment or missing a payment. It is vital that the agreement permits you to remedy this situation with only a modest penalty. Similarly, you should ensure that you have the right to make early repayment (your future financial circumstances may make this a sensible course of action, or you may wish to sell before the end of the mortgage term). Developers' agreements, as with many banking institutions in the United States, often require lenders to pay a penalty for early redemption of the loan, and this should be avoided.

Purchasing dollars for your mortgage repayments

If you are funding a US mortgage from monies abroad then you will have to pay fees both for the exchange of your currency into dollars and for the transfer of the funds to your US account. You should shop around for prices for both, and ensure that you pay a 'commercial' and not a tourist rate for your dollars. Generally you will receive a less expensive service from specialist currency dealers, rather than the main banks.

Stop worrying about the cost of buying Dollars

STOP

Start talking to the experts!

SGM-FX offers a friendly and commission-free service to ensure you secure the best possible exchange rate when converting your funds into Dollars.

Contact us:

UK tel: +44 (0) 20 7778 0123
Email: info@sgm-fx.com
Web: www.sgm-fx.com

BUYING PROPERTY IN FLORIDA? THOUGHT ABOUT THE EXCHANGE RATE?

Foreign Exchange Rates will have a significant impact on the cost of your purchase.

In securing property abroad, purchasers are likely to spend more time searching for the right property via their estate agent and researching the best method of financing their purchase rather than considering the financial implications of transferring money overseas. Unfortunately the majority of people do not think about the exchange rate until the last minute. This leaves the buyer exposed to the prevailing exchange rate and can significantly alter the eventual cost of the property.

When buying abroad it is essential to cover all aspects of the currency element of the transaction. For example, when considering the dollar cost of purchasing a house in Florida there is no fixed exchange rate from which to calculate the eventual cost in sterling. This is because the foreign exchange rate changes constantly, all day, every day. For example, (at the time of writing this article) in the last seven months alone, the GBP/USD rate has fluctuated between 1.9475 dollars to the pound and 1.7505. Putting this into perspective, if you are buying a $300,000 property in Florida, this is a fluctuation of just under £17,500! A noticeable difference for anyone!

THE SOLUTION

SGM-Foreign Exchange aims to take away the worry of your foreign currency transaction. By consulting with SGM-FX the buyer has access to a Personal Account Manager who will guide you through the process and discuss the most beneficial time and way to transfer funds. As currency experts, we have access to the inter-bank market (wholesale prices) allowing you to make significant savings on your overseas purchase. Not only that, SGM-FX will also be able to alert you to any positive or negative movements enabling you the greater opportunity of buying at the peak rather than the low.

OTHER BENEFITS

Our facilities not only include the ability to buy or sell currency for same day delivery at the best available rate, but also the opportunity to secure an excellent rate for up to 12 months in advance. This is done by arranging a forward price for your currency based upon the current exchange rate.

Buying currency forward gives you the opportunity to secure a favourable exchange rate for a future date. For example, if you have a tight budget to work towards, you can secure the rate knowing that you can afford your property no matter where the exchange rate goes afterwards. Buying forward completely eliminates the risk that the markets will drop and force you to spend more than you can actually afford.

SGM-FX is able to offer you an advantage to dealing with banks both in terms of cost and service. We have a wealth of experience and will make that available to you in a clear and friendly manner. Simply by talking with SGM-Foreign Exchange you are giving yourself the opportunity to secure a better rate in addition to a first class service by currency experts.

Written by SGM-Foreign Exchange Ltd. 0207 778 0123 info@sgm-fx.com

www.sgm-fx.com

FABB: The Florida Association of British Business

You will find a list of British businesses operating in Florida, including financial advisers, who are accustomed to advising expatriates, especially British and Irish. They can assist those needing a mortgage but who do not have a US credit history. See the website **www.BritishFlorida.com**.

For a dictionary of mortgage terms go to **www.mortgageguide101.com/ glossary**.

For further information it is worthwhile purchasing *The Mortgage Money Guide*. This is available from the Federal Trade Commission free of charge. The address is 600 Pennsylvania Avenue, NW, Washington, DC 20580–0002.

6 Buying a new property and having a property built

The construction industry in Florida is thriving, thanks in part to a continual demand for housing from many foreign buyers anxious to secure their home in the sun. A new property has obvious attractions. It is clean and bright. You are the first occupier. There are no renovation works to put up with, yet you have the freedom to choose your own colour schemes and materials, and can generally agree some variations to the builders' basic plan. The property will invariably have double glazing, up-to-date insulation, central heating, good ventilation and good security. Those who are the first to purchase on the development will have considerable choice as to their location on the site. Furthermore, most developments include at least some amenities, with many boasting a complex with various sports and other facilities, as well as a swimming pool.

There are disadvantages! A major one is that you have to finance the purchase for a year or more before you can move in, and whilst you are still funding the cost of your existing living accommodation. A second drawback is that despite the size of your investment, you will almost certainly have to buy it unseen ('off plan'), though you may be able to inspect a show house. A reputable developer will often have sold all the properties on a development before work has even commenced. Indeed, in the most popular areas, you should be wary of purchasing on a development that is nearly completed but that has a number of properties still unsold. This may be because the price is particularly high, or because there is something unsatisfactory about the site or the developer that has caused others not to purchase. Invariably you will have to wait over a year for construction to be completed. A third disadvantage relates to possible inadequacies in the construction of your new home.

One sensible approach is to choose a selection of builders that are known to be reputable and solvent, and to choose from their selection of properties. Do not buy from a builder about whom you know nothing. Take the trouble to talk to owners in the developments in which you are considering purchasing, or in a recently constructed development by the same builder. Even though you are buying a new property, follow the advice in Chapter 4 on instructing a surveyor or home inspector. If you are purchasing off plan ask the inspector to look at other properties currently being built by the same constructor – this may well provide more enlightening information than could be obtained that from the survey of a completed property!

You might also ask questions about the reputation of various developers from local estate agencies, consumer groups or especially the local planning and building departments. You need to know, in particular, how long a company has been constructing houses, and its reputation for quality and for meeting construction times. Note that many developers advertise properties at very low prices to attract interest, but when you enter into detailed discussions you will often find that many features that you might expect to be standard are in fact 'optional' additions, and can increase the cost of the house by as much as 25 per cent or even more. You should ensure that it is very clear what is and what is not included in the price that you are going to pay. It is also possible to negotiate substantial reductions in relation to these extras – the builder's profit margin on these items is often huge, and far greater than his return on the house that he has constructed. Insist that the make and model of items included in the sale are specified, otherwise the developer will almost certainly install cheaper 'equivalents'.

Only purchase from a developer that offers a new house warranty backed by an independent insurance company. As a minimum the warranty should cover major structural defects over 10 years, plumbing, electrical, heating systems and air-conditioning systems for two years and 12 months for workmanship and materials. You or your lawyer should check on the financial health of the developer and the details of insurance cover should the builder go into liquidation, or otherwise fail to complete the building. Remember that if something sounds too good to be true, it probably is not true. Always read the contract with care (see below for the standard terms that it should contain), and ensure that any promises or representations made to you by the developer's representative are included in the contract before you sign. Any alterations after signature should be recorded in writing.

"If only we'd done it sooner!"

At the Florida Store, this is the phrase we hear most from the many British people who choose to buy their own luxury villa in Orlando. Whether it's from a family starting to enjoy their twice yearly holidays in the sun, a retired couple appreciating the warm winters and low cost of living or the shrewd investor who has already seen the value of his property increasing, the comment remains the same. And the good news is that it's not too late to join them; villa prices continue to rise at around 2% per month and even homes that have already been occupied for several years are snapped up as soon as they come on to the market. The Orlando property boom continues!

The reasons for this continuing popularity are many, but the ongoing growth of the Orlando area is key. Not only are holiday-makers enjoying ever-increasing facilities but so are business conventions; Orlando is now the established convention capital of the world. Large corporations are also taking advantage of the climate and cost of living index, and the business district of Orlando is expanding apace. All of this means a very healthy future for the area, and with over 50 million visitors per year, an equally healthy demand for short-term villa rental. But what initially attracts most people to buy in Orlando is the extraordinary value for money. A fully furnished luxury pool home in a good location is often cheaper than a suburban semi-detached in the UK.

The best way to join the homeowners of Orlando is to buy "off plan" with a locked-in price. Many of the builders we work with will hold your chosen lot – and more importantly, the price – for up to 60 days with just a $1,000 *refundable* deposit. Depending on the builder, you may only need 10% of the purchase price to go to contract, with the remaining deposit not needed until completion. For the wise buyer this offers tremendous investment potential; you are only paying the minimum deposit but yet enjoying the property appreciation on the full price of the home. Due to demand, villa property is generally taking an average of 18 months or even two years to build, but the home can have gone up in value by an average of 50% in that time – even before you receive the keys! Compare that to UK property, or to a holiday home in Europe and the advantages are clear.

With so many companies willing to sell you a property in Orlando, buyers may feel that it doesn't much matter which one they go with. It does! Not all companies or agents offer both purchase assistance and the ongoing maintenance and rental income that is so essential to most British buyers. There are hundreds of realty agents in Orlando who, along with a Title Company, will handle the legal process of transferring ownership of property from seller to buyer. But after the sale the best you can expect is to be sign-posted to a management company willing to take you on their books, or you may have to look around yourselves.

At the Florida Store, we offer a seamless integrated service that pays as much attention to your villa after the sale as before. We have invested in offices in both the UK and Orlando and employ a dedicated team of specialists covering everything from the initial buying process, licensed realtors to process the sale, mortgages, immigration, through to full home management. We operate one of the industry's most comprehensive marketing programmes to ensure healthy rental income for all our property owners. Many people who have bought their villas elsewhere would like to have us carry out their management and rental needs, but the service is exclusive to customers of the Florida Store.

If you're considering buying a dream home in Orlando, make the Florida Store your first call on **01388 813378**. Better still, come along to one of our nationwide shows, where our friendly and experienced staff will can tell you everything you want to know.

Information on our roadshow dates and places, together with much other useful information can be found on our website www.floridastore.uk.com

Meet the
DREAM TEAM

We've been helping people buy their dream home in the sun for over ten years. Not only buy it, but to service it, maintain it, and generate its important rental income.

Doing this to the highest standards demands a team of experienced people who really know the area and care about their clients. The Florida Store.

The result is hundreds of satisfied customers in the UK who not only enjoy regular free holidays in their luxury homes, but can relax knowing their investment is being properly looked after and paying its way.

- *Friendly, unbiased advice*
- *Total support throughout the purchase process*
- *Licensed Realtors*
- *Two offices in Greater Orlando plus the UK and Europe*

Call us now on:
0800 1696 247
or visit one of our nationwide shows
(see website for details)

THE FLORIDA STORE

www.floridastore.uk.com

www.floridainvestmenthomesuk.com

- Finest quality luxury buy-to-let pool homes available in Kissimmee, Florida
- Close to all major attractions
- Unique UK $ mortgage facility with UK processing
- New build and resale available
- Tax and mortgage advise
- Management and rental
- Properties available from 20% deposit
- UK and Florida sales office – no pressure selling, just good honest advice to help you find the right home
- **Thinking of selling?**

We have clients on our waiting list ready to buy

Free Phone 0800 018 2442

Online information request and mortgage pre-approval Exchange rate has never been so good –
buy now and actually save money

www.floridainvestmenthomesuk.com

Florida Villa Interiors by U.K. couple

House purchasing is known to be one of the most stressful activities in our lives today. If this is coupled with unfamiliar property laws and currency exchange rate considerations, due to the purchase being in a foreign country, your ideal purchase can become complicated with limited time and space to maneuver. (*A major stress alert* waiting in the wings.)

After your completion date you breathe a sigh of relief, only to remember that it is a beautiful, but very empty property. Where do you begin when your property needs to be furnished to a standard that will be compatible with (and excel) the current rental markets needs, and so attractive that your guests will want to return?

The British owners of Florida Villa Interiors Inc. formed the company with the vision to make home ownership in Florida a rewarding experience. The company aim to support owner's dreams of a tastefully furnished, cost effective home by securing sound relationships with clients and offering a high quality service; before, during and after sales are complete.

Florida Villa Interiors Inc. is a bit of magic you need at a crucial time! An associate will discuss your furnishing needs and help you to select furniture and accessories with the rental climate and your budget in mind. The company offers a complete 'Turn Key' service, the company will deliver, unpack, set furniture out, assemble items, and remove all packaging. Your home will be ready to use by you as the owner or by a guest and will furnish your home so that you and your guests stress-free vacation begins the moment you put the key in the door.

The company has an expert window treatment consultant whose work has been featured in the 'Parade of Homes' and some of the model homes. The floral artist works with a wide range of artificial greenery and flowers and can design a complementary arrangement for any home.

Review some testimonials from previous clients whose dreams have been realized with our help:

'...with their advice and guidance...proven to be an elegant and stylish package...'
Mr. and Mrs. Kavanagh, Galway, Ireland

'...excellent service...impressed with your ideas.'   *Mr. Bleach Caterham, Surrey*

'...professionalism...our house looked like it belonged in a glossy magazine...'
Mr. and Mrs. Taylor, South Yorkshire, United Kingdom

Allow Florida Villa Interiors Inc. to help you realize your dreams of a tastefully furnished trouble-free vacation home.

THE REAL FLORIDA SPECIALISTS

A selection of our current Florida developments. We also have plenty of resale opportunities in Florida - visit our website for more details.

Bella Barcelona

- Exclusive development of just 108 units
- Courtyard pool and spa feature
- Fully furnished
- Games Rooms
- 12 month **guaranteed** rental programme
- Close to major parks
- Phase one units just released

Coming Soon . . .

Miami

- Selection of Condo conversion hotels
- High capital growth and occupancy
- Art deco/renaissance period
- Boutiques, shops and fantastic lifestyle
- Own beach club
- Strong management company

Coral Cay

- 156 townhomes with spas
- Located just off 192
- Fully furnished
- Guaranteed rental available
- Clubhouse and facilities on site
- Gated community

Harborlights Resort

- Off-plan development, early investor incentives
- Pre-approved mortgage funding
- 40 minutes from Disney
- All condoniums have a view of Lake Haines
- On-site attractions and facilities - including private beach
- Access to parks, golf courses and watersports
- Great rental potential
- Region of high capital growth - over 18% in the past year
- Inclusive top quality furniture package

Win one of our FREE holidays to sunny Florida - visit us on stand N38 at A Place in the Sun Live 2005 for more details

The property specialists you can trust

For more information, visit us at Stand N38 at A Place in the Sun Live, 30 September - 2 October 2005, ExCel, London and WIN the chance for a FREE Florida holiday*

For distribution in the UK only

THE PROPERTY SPECIALISTS
YOU CAN TRUST

World Property Centre (WPC) has been helping individuals realise their overseas property dreams for over a decade now. In its early days, the company operated under trading names emphasising its Florida connections; however, over the past five years WPC has developed into a truly worldwide company offering property for sale in North and South America, the Caribbean, Europe and even in Dubai.

The company now employs over 50 staff and has offices in Europe, the USA and in Canada.

What is the reason for WPC's enormous growth? Primarily, it is the company's commitment to quality of service to its clients. The objective of many overseas property sales companies is simply to achieve the sale; World Property Centre has invested in a complete "one stop shop" approach. In addition to identifying good investment opportunities, the company also has a number of Divisions offering advice on everything from mortgages to visa, immigration and relocation services, as well as on property rental services. Indeed, such is the company's relationship with some major tour operators that it is even able to offer **guaranteed rental programmes** on some developments. These Divisions are supported by an in-house Sales Support Team dedicated to guiding clients through the whole process.

There is one external influence on the Company's success: the poor performance of stocks and shares over recent years. WPC searches carefully for opportunities for investors to place their money into bricks and mortar in areas where there is a proven track record of high appreciation rates. A recent project showed investors **over 100% return** in just eighteen months, achieved by negotiating early investment bonuses for those purchasing "off plan".

So if you are thinking of expanding your investment portfolio to include overseas property, or are just looking for that second home that will generate some income when you are not using it, World Property Centre can help. They really are **the property specialists you can trust**.

For more information visit **www.worldpropertycentre.com** or call them on **01268 286500**.

The details set out in Chapter 4 relating to the purchase of your property are of general application, and for the most part apply also to the purchase of a new property, and to having a property built.

Buying a plot of land and having a house built for you is invariably much cheaper than buying a house built by a developer. Whether you are buying from a developer or purchasing a building plot, you should pay particular attention to the terrain and the matters set out in Chapter 4 under the heading 'Viewing the property'.

Building plots

If you are building your own house, or having a house built, then it is imperative that you find yourself a good lawyer, and a good architect. You must also be prepared to devote a lot of time in personal supervision of the works, at least if you want the outcome to correspond to what you had in mind at the outset.

The land you buy may already form part of a developed area with services already arranged and with the benefit of planning permission, or may be totally without services or any planning permission. In either case, give consideration to the nature of the underlying surface – it could have a major impact on the costs of construction. The key to ascertaining the nature of the land is to ask as many questions as you can, not merely from the vendor, but also of neighbours and at the local council. Above all, have an expert examine the land.

It is particularly important to take note of what you see on the ground. Be alert to any signs of a path running across the plot, which may be a right of way, and also to the boundaries.

If you are having your own property built you are all the more in need of help and guidance from lawyers and other experts. Obviously, help and guidance from someone who has already had their own home built, especially in the same locality, and who can come with you to the local council's town planning department, can be invaluable. You also need to check on the building regulations which dictate such matters as how high you can build, how close to the boundary you can construct the house, the height of any boundary wall, etc.

Remember that the information obtained prior to your purchase is merely a snapshot of the situation at a particular point in time. If there is land near to your property that has not been developed, you might find that the land becomes yet another construction site on which a property will be built that may not be to your liking, and may affect your view and the value of your property. This is simply a risk you take, unless you purchase a remaining plot of land in an area already well developed.

The land may already have planning permission. You will need to check carefully what is permitted, and any conditions attached to the permission. If there is no planning permission, you will need to factor the cost of obtaining this into your calculations. If you are concerned that there is a risk of planning permission being refused, and you are being pressed to commit yourself and do not want to risk this plot slipping through your fingers, ask your lawyer about having a condition in the contract that enables you to avoid the contract if an expert advises that the land will be expensive, difficult or impossible to build on.

If the plot is not connected to the various services, you should check if there are likely to be any problems with connecting to the mains water and mains sewerage, gas, electricity and telephone networks. Even if these services extend to neighbouring properties, you will almost certainly bear the costs of connecting to the networks. Check on access to the property, including access for works vehicles that will need to deliver supplies or carry out works at the property during construction. Also, if the boundaries are not already fenced, the contract of sale is likely to require you to erect fencing at your expense.

Besides the option of instructing an architect to design a property, there are companies that offer a range of standard properties that they will construct for you and to which they will make internal modifications to suit your requirements. If this option appeals, ask to see examples of properties already constructed by the company. You need to be absolutely certain what is included in the price, in particular in relation to fittings in the kitchen and bathroom, as well as the garage and garden. This is obviously a cheaper option than the individually architect-designed route and, as the companies have often constructed their models with the approach of the local planning authorities in mind, you should be less likely to encounter problems from that quarter.

Employing an architect will obviously increase the costs of construction. He or she will normally prepare the (detailed) list of specifications. This will indicate the nature and quality (and hence cost) of the materials to be used in the construction of your house. You will obviously need to discuss this with the architect in some detail. This will form the basis of any builder's bid to do the work. While it would be advisable to obtain several bids, your architect should be able to help you choose which builders to invite to bid, and which of the bids to accept. The architect's fees will obviously be determined in part by the extent to which he or she oversees the progress of the construction and verifies that it complies with the various building regulations.

The building contract

Whether you buy a property from a developer, purchase the land yourself and purchase a standard building package, or instruct an architect and builder to design and build a house for you, the building contract should contain the following standard terms:

- the total cost, to include all necessary certificates and licences;
- a detailed description and plan of the property to be built;
- the quality of the materials to be used;
- a schedule of construction and ancillary work;
- the completion date and penalty clauses for late completion of the work (and late payment by yourself);
- insurance cover during the period of construction;
- the deposit and stage payments;
- (ideally) a term stating that a percentage (say 5 per cent) of the contract price should be withheld for several months as a guarantee should any problems appear.

Once the building work is finished, you must take a careful look at the contract to ensure that every detail is covered, from doors and windows, to kitchen, bathroom and toilet fittings, to wall and floor finishes. Do not be surprised if the work takes longer than envisaged. The developer is bound to hit some problem or other and is allowed some leeway to complete the task. Do visit the construction site from time to time to satisfy yourself that matters are proceeding properly and raise any concerns that you have. An error in the construction can be much more easily and speedily corrected if identified at an early stage.

After completion of the work, you and a representative of the developer should meet together to ensure that you are happy with the work that has been carried out. I strongly recommend that you instruct a surveyor or architect to inspect the property on your behalf at this point. It is the occasion when you can make a record of anything that is not as it should be. If the property does not correspond to your expectations as set out in the contract, then a list should be recorded (a snag list) of what is missing or faulty. Do not close escrow (ie pay over the outstanding monies to complete your purchase) unless you are satisfied that everything is correct, or at least have a written record signed by the developer of the outstanding items that he is to attend to, and the timescale in which he will carry this out. If you need to move in, but the outstanding work is significant, you should insist that a proportion of what you are to pay the developer is put in a separate trust account following completion of the purchase, and that the developer agrees in writing that these monies should only be released to him after satisfactory and timely completion of the outstanding works, failing which you will be free to use the funds to instruct another party to do so. If the developer refuses, at the very least have a signed record of the work he has acknowledged has not been correctly carried out. This is an important piece of evidence should you need to bring a claim in the courts.

Useful contacts and addresses

Florida Home Builders Association, PO Box 1259, Tallahassee, FL 32302, tel: (850) 224 4316, **www.fhba.com**
Homebuilder: **www.homebuilder.com**
Lennars (one of largest and oldest builders in Florida): **www.lennar.com**

Buying an apartment or private property in a condominium; timeshares and mobile homes

There are over 1 million condominium properties (often referred to as 'condos') in Florida. A condominium is a popular form of community ownership, common in apartment blocks, or modern developments, especially in city centres or coastal areas where the supply of land is limited. Each proprietor owns the private parts of his or her apartment or house, but the common parts, including lifts, hallways and stairs, the entranceway to the building, the approach road, gardens, pathways and so on, are owned in common. These are maintained by a 'board of administration' elected by the proprietors.

These properties are often more affordable and offer owners a number of advantages, including often a higher level of security, easy maintenance and less responsibility than if they owned a separate dwelling. Developments frequently have facilities such as pools and gardens, and even shopping centres, that you can enjoy without the inconvenience and burden of the extra maintenance required.

On the other hand, you have less privacy, are more at risk from disturbance by your neighbours and can be subject to large service charges/community fees over which you have little control. In some instances, factions can develop with deep animosity between owners, and arguments erupting about every conceivable detail of how the development should be run.

In holiday resorts, you may find that the communal swimming pool or sports facilities are so overloaded at peak times as to be of no benefit.

Accordingly, if you are purchasing a resale as opposed to a new property, you would do well to make your initial visit during the peak season and ask what restrictions are placed on the use of such facilities.

Before agreeing to buy such an apartment or home, it is imperative that you ask to see the rules governing the development. Indeed, a person selling a condominium is required to provide interested purchasers with a set of documents prior to the signature of a contract. These documents include the rules and regulations governing the smooth running of the development, information about the financial state of the development, and any claims brought by or against the association running it. The development's internal regulations will govern what you can and cannot do. They may prohibit you from exercising any business or profession; impose restrictions on renting; prohibit the keeping of pets; or impose a uniform colour scheme on awnings and restrict external alterations to your property. These rules also set out what is covered by the service charges and how the cost of these is to be divided.

You should ask to see the minutes of the last two or three Annual General Meetings to see what issues were discussed. These and the other documents disclosed should give you an idea of any problems associated with the development, and of any significant expenditure that is on the horizon.

You should also see the receipts for the last two or three years' services charges. You need to see these, not only to ensure that they have been paid by the vendor, but also because they will give you an idea of the charges that you will have to pay if you purchase. The charges include the costs of maintaining, repairing, cleaning, lighting, heating and insuring the common parts and the administration involved for the development. All proprietors have to pay a share of these costs in accordance with the proportionate size of their property, and usually irrespective of whether or not they make use of the facilities. There is generally no rebate if your property is unoccupied for prolonged periods of time, so take care if you are looking for a holiday apartment. Note that garage and parking facilities often have to be purchased separately.

You would be especially well advised when considering the purchase of such a property to introduce yourself to neighbours if the opportunity arises or can be created. A very short conversation may immediately warn you off, and a longer conversation may reveal problems with the management of the development that at least require questions to be asked by you and/or your lawyer. Ask them bluntly 'Would you buy again?'!

Look carefully at the condition of the development. Are any major expenses likely to be required in the near future? Ask your lawyer to ask the vendor whether he or she knows of any impending expenditure.

Note that Florida law provides purchasers of condominiums with a 15-day cooling-off period, during which they can cancel the agreement. For obvious reasons the cancellation must be in writing. Further information about purchasing a condominium in Florida can be obtained from the Division of Florida Land Sales, Condominiums and Mobile Homes, tel: (850) 488 1122.

Timeshares

Timeshare schemes remain fairly popular in Florida. In a timeshare scheme the purchaser buys the right to the use of the property for a limited period each year, often only a week or two. There are two types of timeshare: the 'interval ownership' and the 'right to use'.

An interval ownership purchaser has the right to sell, rent out, or give away his or her share. With a right to use the buyer gains *no* legal interest in the property. The price of buying either form of timeshare is understandably much less than purchasing a holiday home, as are the maintenance costs. The developer, on the other hand, invariably makes a much higher profit than on a usual sale, as he or she will probably only have to sell a few weeks' use of the property to break even. Further, the service company responsible for the management of the development generally succeeds in levying much higher charges than on a normal development. With charges for each apartment shared between several 'owners', the timeshare owners tend to pay the over-inflated rates, rather than entering into conflict with the service company and risk losing their allocated time.

Most timeshare agreements are entered into during a 'presentation' when the prospective purchaser is subjected to extremely 'hard sell'. In the past, once he or she had signed, the purchaser had no opportunity to escape from the agreement; the contract was entirely weighted in favour of the developer and the service company. Fortunately regulations have been introduced, including a 10-day cooling-off period. You are entitled, as a matter of law, to cancel at any time during that period without any financial cost, and to have the deposit you paid refunded in full (within two days of giving notification of cancellation).

While buying a timeshare is much cheaper than purchasing your own apartment or house, you should nevertheless seriously consider consulting a lawyer before signing any agreement. The new regulations provide considerable protection, but the operators of timeshare companies are constantly making changes to their schemes in an effort to avoid the regulations, and the law is often too slow to keep up. These efforts often include conjuring up new names for their schemes, with such terms as 'vacation plans' and 'holiday ownership' now in current usage.

Whilst many timeshares offer you flexibility and allow you to exchange time in 'your' apartment for time in an apartment in another timeshare development elsewhere in the world, in practice it may be rather more difficult and more expensive to exchange than you were led to believe. Note also that usually it is not at all easy to sell a timeshare, and even if you succeed you are unlikely to have made a profit, and may have to sell at a substantial loss.

Before considering a timeshare purchase, at the very least consult the Timeshare Consumers' Association website at **www.timeshare.org.uk** or telephone them on 01909 591 100.

Mobile homes

There are well over 1 million mobile homes in Florida. They are significantly cheaper than other forms of property and accordingly remain popular, despite the devastating damage inflicted on so many mobile home parks by recent hurricanes. You can obtain further information from the Division of Florida Land Sales, Condominiums and Mobile Homes, tel: (850) 488 1122.

8 Settling in

Florida is a popular location for people who are retired or planning their retirement, or who want to purchase a holiday home. It is hardly a surprising choice given the weather in the Sunshine State, and the low housing costs. Note, however, that whilst the possibility of a right to residence based solely on retirement has been listed for consideration for some time, there is at present no such right. Unless you can qualify for a visa enabling you to stay for some time (see Chapter 12 on Immigration into the United States), you will be limited to stays of three months at a time.

In practice, the UK property market and the present exchange rate have meant that many British citizens have been able to afford to invest in a business in Florida and thereby obtain an E-2 visa, often in addition to being able to purchase a very comfortable home.

It is important, however, to be realistic, for it is retired expatriates who are the most likely to return home. Consider what you are likely to miss in the UK or Canada, whether you are likely to feel at home in Florida, how you will manage with the different culture and how you will cope with advancing age and possible illness and the loss of a partner.

If, after considering these aspects, you are determined to make the move, or simply to buy a holiday home, there are several areas, in particular in the south of Florida, where much of what you may miss about life in the UK or Canada is duplicated, including for Britons cricket, the great British pub, and British food. The most popular areas tend to be the most expensive, but you may find them more conducive to making a home and developing a feeling of belonging.

Retiring to Florida

There is no problem with receiving UK state and private pensions in Florida, which can be paid into a US bank account. Those already in receipt of a British state pension should note that it can take up to four months for the arrangements to be made for them to have their pension paid in the United States. You should contact your local Benefits Agency before leaving the UK. For further information see the website **www.dwp.gov.uk/lifeevent/penret/index.asp**. Advice to pensioners is available from various organizations, including Help the Aged, and in relation specifically to pensions, on the website **www.Ukfrozenpensions.com**. Payment of widow's benefit can be arranged in the same way as a retirement pension. You can obtain information on war pensions from the Ministry of Defence: Veterans Agency Tomlinson House, Norcross, Norcross Lane, Thornton-Cleveleys FY5 3WP. Tel: 0800 169 2277. E-mail: help@veteransagency.gsi.gov.uk; **www.veteransagency.mod.uk**.

If you have not yet retired, your existing entitlement to a UK pension will be frozen and you will receive a reduced pension from the UK authorities when you reach retirement age. For those approaching retirement, it may be worthwhile making voluntary payments to bring your National Insurance contributions up to the level entitling you to a full pension. You should contact the Pension Service's International Pension Centre (part of the Department for Work and Pensions, a renamed part of the former DSS, on tel: 0191 218 7777) and the Inland Revenue's Centre for Non-Residents (tel: 0845 070 0040) to ask for up-to-date information and advice, including whether you should pay Class 2 or Class 3 contributions. The former is the more expensive option but entitles you to incapacity benefit.

One matter that you do need to consider is exchange rate fluctuations. You could move some of your investments to the United States. Alternatively, you could just accept that there is a risk that sterling may suffer modest falls in value, and discuss with your financial adviser how quickly you could move your investments if it was felt that sterling was likely to become particularly weak. Issues relating to inheritance are covered in Chapter 14.

Payment of other UK benefits while living in Florida

Those currently in receipt of an old-age pension, invalidity and disability benefits, widow's benefits or benefits received as a result of an accident at work, or an occupational disease, are entitled to have their benefits paid to them irrespective of where they choose to live. Attendance Allowance and

Disability Living Allowance are not normally payable once you move abroad permanently. The relevant benefits should be paid gross and include any increases. Incapacity benefit will only be paid to those who have paid Class 1 or Class 2 and 4 National Insurance contributions.

There is also an agreement between the United States and the UK governing social security payments (ask for Leaflet SA33, and/or see the website **www.dss.gov.uk**). Further information can also be obtained from the Overseas Benefits Directorate, Department of Social Security Benefits, Agency, Tyneview Park, Whitley Road, Benton, Newcastle-upon-Tyne NE98 1BA, tel: 191 218 7777, fax: 191 218 7293, e-mail: baadmin@ baadmin.demon.co.uk.

Paying National Insurance Contributions

US residents wishing to continue UK National Insurance Contributions in order to maintain eligibility to certain benefits should contact the Inland Revenue, National Insurance Contributions Office, International Services, Room A2119, Longbenton, Newcastle Upon Tyne NE98 1ZZ England, tel: (from outside the UK) 44 191 2254811, tel: (from the UK) 0645 154811.

Importing your belongings

Visitors and non-residents are permitted to import articles for their own personal use free of any duty, including items such as furniture and household items. For motor vehicles see Chapter 9. Items that are shipped must go through customs on arrival in the United States. Reputable removal companies are familiar with the correct procedures and necessary form filling, details of which can also be seen at **www.customes.ustreas.gov**, the website of the US customs. You will also find useful information, and names of removal companies, at **www.britsintheus.com**. Always obtain a written estimate, and take special care to ensure that your belongings are properly and adequately insured. Many people find that they receive better value cover by taking out their own insurance, rather than that of the removal company.

If you are taking a computer with you, you will need a step-down transformer, unless one is already incorporated into your machine. Florida has similar restrictions to the UK in relation to importing such items as drugs

and firearms. There are also regulations relating to the importing of animals, animal products, plants and items with a possible military use. If in doubt, you should ask for advice from United States customs.

Pets

To import a cat or dog from either the UK or Canada into the United States you will simply require an official certificate of veterinary inspection from your local vet, though you should have your dog vaccinated against rabies. The certificate is to confirm that your animal does not have any indications of an infectious or communicable disease, has no history of exposure to any animal infected with rabies and does not come from an area under quarantine for rabies. There are special regulations governing the importation of collies or sheepdogs arising out of the use of these breeds for managing livestock. You can find information relating to the importing of pets at the website of the US Department of Agriculture, **www.aphis.usda.gov**, and of your local US embassy or consulate.

If you wish to bring a dog or cat into, or back into, the UK you will need to have your pet fitted with a microchip and then vaccinated against rabies. A microchip can be painlessly inserted. I have been assured by several vets that the microchips do not irritate dogs. You will then have to arrange to have a blood test to check that the vaccine has been effective and obtain a veterinary certificate. *However, you will have to wait a period of six months after a satisfactory blood test before your pet can enter the UK.* The reason given by the British authorities for this delay is that the vaccine would not protect an animal infected with rabies *before* vaccination, and it takes six months for most infected animals to display any clinical signs of the disease.

Animals not meeting all the rules must be sent into quarantine. If vaccinated *before* the microchip was fitted, your pet will have to be vaccinated again, otherwise the authorities cannot be certain that it was correctly identified when vaccinated. Your pet will also need booster vaccinations within the time stated on the passport or veterinary certificate, or PETS certificate, which must be recorded on the vaccination record and passport. If your pet does not receive the boosters on time, then it will have to be vaccinated and its blood tested again. You will then have to wait six months from the date the new blood sample was taken.

The whole procedure takes about eight months, so you will need to plan ahead. Check with the centre that is to test your animal's blood how long they are currently taking to return results (there is a wide variation). Just before leaving (24–48 hours prior to departure), you will need to have your pet treated by a vet for ticks and tapeworm, the details of which (including the date and time of treatment and the product used) the vet must record on the EU pet passport or the third country official veterinary certificate.

In addition to the certificate, when you travel you must have with you your pet's original vaccination record and blood test result (or certified copies) which show the microchip number. Your pet must travel to the UK and must enter the UK using an approved transport company and route. There are relatively few companies that have made arrangements permitting them to bring pets into the UK (a list is contained in the Appendices). More routes are anticipated in the coming years and you should contact DEFRA (see below) for information. Those bringing a pet into the UK from the United States will need to complete customs formalities. This can be done by a travel agent, travel company or airline but there may be a charge for this.

Similar rules apply to the importation of ferrets into the UK, that is, they must be microchipped, vaccinated against rabies and issued with a passport, and be treated against ticks and tapeworm. This should be recorded on the passport. In the case of ferrets, however, there is no need to wait six months. As to pet rabbits and rodents (such as guinea pigs, hamsters, rats, mice and gerbils), there are at present no requirements for these pets when entering or returning to the UK or any other EU member state, not even in relation to rabies. The EU may in future impose regulations. New EU regulations also cover other animals, including birds (other than poultry), ornamental tropical fish, most invertebrates, and reptiles. At the time of writing, the rules to be passed under this regulation were not yet available. Up-to-date information will be posted on the DEFRA website.

In the UK passports are issued by Part 2 Local Veterinary Inspectors. Further information is obtainable from the Pets Helpline at the Department for Environment Food and Rural Affairs (DEFRA), tel: 08459 335577. There is also a website explaining the procedures at **www.defra.gov.uk** and which contains useful information in relation to the EU generally, but in particular the UK, Ireland and Sweden. Another website worth visiting is that of QUAFF (Quarantine Abolition Fighting

Fund) at **www.dip.demon.co.uk**, tel: 01243 264173. One company specializing in the transport of animals is Animals by Air Ltd, tel: 0870 8338020.

The regulations and a pet passport can be downloaded from the EU website, via **www.defra.gov.uk**. The pet passport contains details of the owner and of the animal, including the date it was microchipped and its vaccination record and blood details.

Transitional arrangements: UK PETS certificates were issued up until 30 September 2004 and they will remain effective until their expiration, and accordingly your animal can enter the UK with a valid PETS certificate. If you already have a previous PETS certificate, you can change this for a pet passport. Take your pet's vaccination record to your veterinary surgeon and the date that it was microchipped for him to record the details in section III of the passport.

Useful information in relation to dogs is contained on the website **www.dogsaway.co.uk**.

Your pet in the Sunshine State

Dogs must be licensed. The cost is about $10 and is payable at the local tax collector's office. It is an offence punishable with a steep fine to allow your dog to foul public places, and accordingly you should buy a 'poop-scoop'. Your dog will not be allowed in restaurants or shopping centres, or even on public transport, guide dogs for the blind excepted. There are also restrictions on having pets in many apartment blocks and housing developments.

There are a number of websites that provide pet owners in Florida with advice, help and assistance. **www.peoplewithpets.com** and **www.rentwithpets.org** enable you to search in several Florida cities for accommodation where your pets are welcome and **www.floridapets.net** has lists of places to stay and live that are pet friendly. **www.JaxLostPets.com** is the North Florida site of the Department of Agriculture's Missing Pet Network and at **www.askmary.com/hurricane.htm** you will find information on how to plan for your pet's safety when a hurricane threatens. **www.dogpark.com** lists parks in Florida where you can take your dog. You can find information about pets, including veterinary surgeons, at **www.healthypet.com**, tel: 1 (800) 883 6301.

A Florida bank account

There are two different types of banks in the United States, commercial banks and savings banks.

There are well over 200 different commercial banks operating in Florida, many of them very small and operating in only one or two counties with perhaps only one branch. In the United States there are no national banks with extensive networks as in the UK and continental Europe, partly because until 1997 banks were not permitted to engage in interstate banking. In Florida, Barnett Bank is by far the largest, with branches in most of the 67 counties. There is intense competition between the banks and it is worth shopping around. Many banks offer special terms for those over 55, such as no charges for current accounts and credit cards. If you are considering a smaller bank you should verify its financial health, for example by requesting a report from an organization such as Veribanc (**www.veribanc.com**; tel: 1 (800) 442 2657) that provides different levels of report from around $15 upwards. You should ensure that any bank you propose to use is covered by the Federal Deposit Insurance Corporation, and that you do not hold more than the current amount (presently around $100,000 per person per bank) covered by the federal insurance in any one bank. Ask the bank for confirmation that it comes within the FDIC scheme, and for the present level of cover.

You will need a current account (known as a 'checking' account). A savings account is termed a 'deposit' account. You will need ID and a utility bill to open an account, and probably a social security or tax number. Banks levy a host of different charges, with a wide range of rates amongst the different banks. As a general rule, you will minimize your bank charges if you keep your balance above the bank's minimum, and only use your own bank's cash point. For most current accounts there is no charge for writing cheques, but customers have to buy their cheques, at a cost of around $15 per batch. You will need to produce ID to use a cheque, but even so you will often find that cheques are only accepted if they are from a Florida bank, or only by people to whom you are known. Many businesses do not accept payment by cheque. It is important not to let your account get overdrawn – it is taken more seriously in the United States than in the UK, for example. If a cheque is bounced, the payer is liable to refund the charges levied on the payee by his or her bank. Repeated offenders will find that their bank closes their account. Their names are entered into a national database and they then have difficulties opening an account elsewhere, and in obtaining credit. It is sensible to take out an insurance policy (overdraft protection) to cover you should you become overdrawn. As with all banks, notify your US bank immediately of any loss or suspected theft of your chequebook or card.

Transferring money to and from the United States

If you are likely to make and receive regular transfers abroad, a bank's charges for this service and its exchange rate should be two of the factors you consider when deciding upon your choice of bank. Once you have a Florida bank account, it is easy to make transfers from abroad into your account. UK banks normally tell you that it will take up to five working days. In practice the transfer may be credited more quickly than this, but in some cases it can take longer. Your home bank may make a charge (in the UK around £20–30 per transfer, irrespective of the amount). Ensure that you obtain the commercial rate for transfers. This is much more favourable than the tourist rate. There are no restrictions on moving money into or out of the United States, save that all sums above $10,000 must be declared.

Household insurance

As at home, you should insure your property for its full worth, taking into account the value of the land, but also the cost of demolition and rebuilding. It is surprising just how many people are significantly under-insured. Similarly, with contents, you should insure their full value if you are to be certain of having a claim met in full. Your insurers need to know if the property is vacant for much of the year and if you are letting the property. If this is the case, the premiums will be higher, but failure to notify your insurer of the situation will result in the disallowance of relevant claims. Homeowners' insurance policies normally include casualty insurance (known as public liability insurance in the UK).

In Florida you will need cover for flood and windstorm damage, with reasonably good rates available from the government's National Flood Insurance Programme (see **www.fema.gov/nfip**; tel (813) 975 7451). Wind-only policies are available from Citizens Property Insurance Corporation, **www.citizensfla.com**. Claims normally have to be submitted within a very short time of an incident so you should check the terms of the policy. Thefts and break-ins also have to be reported to the police as a condition of the policy, usually within 24 hours.

Air-conditioning and heating

Summer is extremely hot and humid wherever you are in Florida, and most residents of the Sunshine State regard air-conditioning as essential, with ceiling fans a cheaper alternative. In much of Florida you will need some form of heating during the winter months. The majority of new houses have a combined system for heating and air-conditioning that is thermostatically controlled. Note that many people dislike the dryness of air caused by air-conditioning and purchase humidifiers to add moisture to the air. One advantage of air-conditioning is that it reduces the growth of mildew, especially if left on at a low setting when you are away.

In deciding how to heat your home you also have to consider the present heating system in the property, the costs of installing a new system, the life expectancy of a new system and your estimated consumption. Most of the power companies provide written guidance on how to reduce your heating and air-cooling costs, and will carry out a study of your requirements free of charge. In apartment blocks there is frequently a central heating system, which is paid in whole or in part through your community fees.

Solar energy

Solar energy is renewable, clean, silent and free. Moreover, a system that uses solar energy requires very little maintenance and should last 20 or 30 years. Solar energy is particularly popular for heating water in Austria and Germany. Florida has rather more hours of sunshine and so solar energy is capable of meeting the majority of your needs for heating both your rooms and your water. A major disadvantage is the relatively high installation cost, and for this reason there are relatively few properties that have solar energy installed. A second drawback is that you will need a back-up system (although portable electric radiators may suffice).

Utilities

You have a choice of utility companies for electricity, water and rubbish collection. In some cases you can sign up for service over the telephone, others insist that you visit their offices. Utility companies will often agree to forego a security deposit if you can provide a letter of reference from your current utility company. If you are a non-resident and absent from your property for long periods of time it is sensible to arrange to make payments by direct debit. All utility companies are overseen by Florida's Public Service Commission (**www.psc.state.fl.us**) which is responsible for ensuring fair competition between the utility companies and for investigating complaints by consumers. It has jurisdiction over electricity, gas, water and telecommunications companies.

Electricity

Electricity is a convenient form of heating, especially for smaller flats and coastal properties in the south where your heating requirements will be very modest. It has the great advantage of being easy and inexpensive to install, so it is often the choice of landlords. The disadvantage of electricity, however, is that the running costs are high.

There are several electricity companies in Florida. The voltage in the United States is 120 volts (compared to 240 volts in the UK). Many electrical appliances purchased in Europe are not suitable for use in the United States, unless they have an internal converter. You will find some useful information on the website **www.fpl.com/** Florida Power and Light.

Water bills

Each consumer is metered separately, and so you pay according to how much water you use. An average family can easily use about 500 litres of water per day. About 60 per cent of an average family's consumption relates to the taking of baths and showers and the flushing of the toilet. Accordingly, substantial reductions in consumption can be made by taking showers instead of baths and choosing the toilet cistern carefully – more modern cisterns use a third or less of the amount used by older toilets. Always check where the main stop-valve or stopcock is located in case you need to turn off the water supply in an emergency. Some parts of the south suffer from occasional droughts.

Communications: the telephone and postal system

In the United States telephone charges are still significantly below the level in most European countries. You have the choice of several telephone companies in Florida, although BellSouth has well over 50 per cent of the market. They all charge a connection fee and deposit costing together around $160. You are not obliged to buy or rent your telephone(s) from your telephone company. Interstate or international calls are provided by a different set of companies, and when you have your telephone connected you will need to select one of these as your provider for such non-local calls. Again the different companies offer a varying range of prices depending on whether the call is interstate or international, and if the latter, the country that is being called. Numbers beginning with 800 are toll-free numbers. These are used by various organizations to permit people to ring from any state without charge. Numbers starting with 700 or 900 involve the caller in paying substantial charges.

If you are renting out your property on short-term lets or your property is empty for several months of the year, you can ask the telephone company to disconnect you during this period, which will reduce your standing charge. One alternative is to leave your telephone available for visitors to your property to make free and local calls without charge. They will then need to use their credit card to make long-distance and international calls. Telephone bills are sent out monthly. It is sensible to arrange for payment of your bills to be by direct debit, to avoid having the line cut off, and perhaps a long wait before it is reactivated. For lowest telephone rates between the UK and the United States see **www.ld.net/calculator/?parlez**.

There is a similar degree of choice when it comes to mobile telephones, both in terms of the number of different companies and the variety of options available with each. You will probably pay less if you chose one of the providers you are using for your fixed line.

First-class mail is generally delivered the next day if locally, and 2–3 days for longer-distance mail. Sending letters by airmail from the United States to the UK normally takes about five working days. You can buy stamps at stationery stores, but you will be charged more than the post office rate.

Here at SBA Interiors, we understand that choosing the perfect furniture for your newly purchased Florida home can be a very stressful experience. There are so many things for you to consider!

Being homeowners ourselves, we have been through the process of choosing furniture with American based furniture package companies, either over the phone or via the internet. It can be exceptionally hard work and most certainly does not suit everyone!

SBA Interiors are here to help you choose your ideal furniture package, personally designed for you, in the comfort of your own home, providing many ideas that will inspire and guide you. It was set up just over 2 years ago after an unpleasant experience with a reputable American furniture package company. We had just purchased a beautiful 5 bed, 3 1/2 bath home and furniture was required to finalise the deal. This was all done rather hurriedly in about 2 hours prior to us leaving for the airport for the return journey home and we felt that we'd simply just run out of time.

This appears to be typical when purchasing a property in Florida. There is always a great deal to do and never enough time to complete the compulsory tasks. We were assured that everything would be taken care of and that we had nothing to worry about.

The end result was OK, but we felt that they hadn't really understood our needs or listened to what we had to say. It was so unbelievably hectic having to focus on a very important part of the buying process whilst keeping another eye on our excited children that we couldn't really remember what we had agreed on! But hey – it was only going to be a rental home so *"what did it matter if it wasn't what we really wanted?"*

However realistically that shouldn't be acceptable and shouldn't be the attitude to take. A lot of money had been spent on our Florida home including the furniture so surely it should look exactly the way we wanted?

That was when SBA Interiors was established. From our experience, we concluded that there would be a demand for a company who could visit you in the comfort of your own home bringing books, catalogues etc and offer you a superior personal service. It would not be the rushed hurried process that we had experienced. We spend time going through each room individually, discussing preferences for colour schemes etc until the whole house is furnished exactly to your requirements. This avoids the American companies' idea of silver, gold and platinum packages.

Once the perfect furniture package is chosen, we arrange a full property survey to ensure everything we have decided on will fit. We then carry out the complete installation right down to the last knife and fork. You do not have to do anything. We take pride in supplying top quality packages at very competitive prices and guarantee the end result will be to your complete satisfaction. All you have to do is take your time and enjoy your perfect Florida home!

To make a perfect start – give us a call on 01634 295405 Mobile: 07801 731735,

visit our website www.sba-interiors.co.uk

or email: info@sba-interiors.co.uk

Television

For many Americans television has become almost a drug, with many US citizens apparently glued to the television for seven to eight hours a day. There is an incredible amount of choice. Unfortunately at least 90 per cent of the output is of incredibly poor quality. Whilst the United States produces the best films in the world, and produces many programmes that are excellent and have proved popular across the world, we are all familiar with the more inferior US television programmes. Once you have watched television in the United States, however, you will appreciate that they keep the worst 90 per cent for domestic viewing only. Europeans who undergo extensive compulsory exposure report feeling as though they have died and gone to hell.

For British residents in Florida, a switch from British to American television can be one of the least attractive features of life in the Sunshine State. However, the BBC has been successful in providing good quality entertainment, education and information across the globe. From the 1970s the BBC has established itself as important force in the US television and publishing marketplace, with 1994 seeing the establishment of BBC Worldwide America, a subsidiary company of BBC Worldwide. BBC America enables those in the United States to have access to the best of British television via a 24-hour US cable channel showing entertainment, sports and news (for more information visit **www.BBCAmerica.com**). The BBC America Shop also gives residents and visitors in the United States access to the best of BBC programmes, videos, books, audio books, CD ROMs, music, toys and games. For more information visit **www.BBCShop.com** and **www.yourbritishshop.com**.

Welcome to Florida

If you wish to integrate fully into Florida life, especially if you live in the more rural areas, you must make contacts among the local community.

There are steps you can take to ease the transition to your new home and environment. Prior to purchasing, or indeed renting, you would do well to introduce yourselves to your immediate neighbours in order to ask them about the property and the neighbourhood. Once you have moved in, renew the acquaintance. You have the perfect pretext in that you are new to the area and can ask them for information or advice about the area or alterations and improvements that they have made to their property.

There will be local sports and cultural associations in which you can participate. If you have children at the local school, you will find that they soon make friends. This will bring you into contact with other parents in the area. Each local school will have its annual events. Integration inevitably requires participation. If you are in a rural area, do carry out some of your shopping locally. Do buy and look at the local newspaper. It is not only about becoming part of the community, but it may be the first notification you have that a new motorway is planned that will directly affect your daily life and/or the value of your property.

There are many British, Scottish, Irish, Welsh and Canadian associations throughout Florida, especially in the more popular areas. They range from churches and religious groups, to cricket clubs, women's groups, activities for children and retired servicemen's associations. You will find a list of some of them on the website **www.sunnybrits.com**. There are also various UK and joint cultural centres and groups – most notably the British Council. Friendships are often quick to form among the expatriate communities. Whatever your age and circumstances, you may find others' help and advice indispensable, including in relation to finding employment. You will find a list of British clubs and associations at the website of the British Consulate in Miami – **www.britainusa.com/miami**. Find in Britain will help you search for any goods or service you require from the UK (see its website: **www.findinbritain.com**). The *Union Jack* newspaper is said to have a readership of 200,000 (see its website at: **www.ujnews.com**).

Information technology help for the over-50s

For the past 20 years SeniorNet Learning Centres have been providing inexpensive computer, word processing and internet classes specifically aimed at adults aged 50 and above. There are also computer courses covering personal financial management and managing your taxation, with various social activities also organized through the centres. The tuition is very much 'hands on' and for the most part provided by volunteer instructors, though the centres often receive sponsorship from charitable foundations or business, including from computer companies. If there is no centre in your area, Seniornet will consider providing help to set one up.

Current locations include Boca Raton, Boynton Beach, Cocoa Beach, Daytona Beach, Orlando, Sarasota, North Miami Beach, Sunrise, Tampa and Vero Beach. For further information consult **www.seniornet.org/**.

Speaking and learning Spanish

In many parts of Florida Hispanics form a sizeable proportion of the local population, and if you are going to go into business may represent an important element of your clientele.

There is no doubt that Spanish is a much easier language than French, the traditional choice of foreign language for most of us in our school days. Florida is an ideal place in which to learn it. There are many different courses. Many courses will be in the target language only (Spanish), with no English spoken. The most well-known organization is the Instituto Cervantes, which is akin to the British Council, or L'Institut Français for France. There are (expensive) total immersion options available in which you spend a period of time in a Spanish family, attending courses during the day.

If you wish to study the language prior to moving to Florida, consider the courses run by the Instituto Cervantes, which has centres in London, Manchester and Dublin. These are cultural centres where you can also learn more about Hispanic culture, see Spanish films and meet Spanish-speaking people living in the UK or Ireland.

Your neighbours and you

The key to minimizing problems is always to attempt to establish a good relationship with your neighbours from the outset, whatever their nationality, even if you are going to keep them at arm's length. At some point, you may well need each other – especially if you live some distance from shops and other facilities. If a dispute does arise, do your utmost to settle disagreements without recourse to the courts, perhaps asking a third party to act as an arbiter. Litigation may only fuel animosities and leave both sides with substantial legal bills.

You have no right to complain about a nuisance that is no more than a norm for the neighbourhood (such as church bells that have been rung for centuries, but which might lead to mental instability if you were unwise enough to purchase the house next door). This is merely a characteristic of the neighbourhood that you are obliged to accept. For abnormal nuisances, however, there are rules and regulations governing such matters as noise and pollution.

Identification

You will need ID for paying by cheque and to claim residents' discounts available at various attractions for those resident in Florida. You obtain this from the office responsible for issuing a driver's licence at a modest cost.

Police forces

There are three different police bodies in Florida – the municipal police, the sheriffs and the Florida Highway Patrol which is responsible for handling accidents and for policing the highway outside the urban areas. Miami and Orlando have their own special Tourist Oriented Police (TOP), whose responsibilities include airports, car hire locations and the beaches. These officers are happy to advise you on the best route for your journey, and can even supply you with a tourist map.

Emergency numbers

Fire, police, ambulance: 911
Lost credit cards:
American Express: 1 (800) 528 4800
Master Card: 1 (800) 826 2181
Visa: 1 (800) 336 8472

Preparing for and dealing with disasters

You can obtain detailed advice on floods, hurricanes, tornados etc from the website of the Federal Emergency Management Agency, www.fema.gov. The information includes the steps you can take to prepare for a disaster, the insurance cover available and dealing with the aftermath. It provides details of previous flooding and hurricane damage.

Consumer complaints

Florida Consumer Services has an A–Z Resource Guide on its website **www.800helpfla.com** which enables consumers to locate the right agency or resource to contact in relation to consumer complaints. For new cars see under 'Florida's Lemon Law' in Chapter 9.

9 You and your car

A car is an essential means of transport in Florida, because of both the enjoyment it can afford and the limited provision of public transport. In much of the Sunshine State the roads are wide and open. Driving along the coast, the views are truly spectacular, though the coastal highways I-75 and I-95 are often blighted with traffic congestion. In much of the more densely populated southern half, especially the tourist areas and built-up urban centres, congestion is a major problem. Avoid built-up and populated areas in the rush hours – and that means 8.00–10.00 am and 4.00–7.00 pm.

Importing your car

In short, unless your car was intended for the US market, this is not only expensive, but administratively complicated, time-consuming and often very frustrating. You will have to go through the Environmental Protection Agency, the Department of Transportation and the US Customs Service as well as the Internal Revenue Service. The vehicle will have to pass various Federal Motor Vehicle Safety Standards, and you may well have to enlist the help of a registered importer to bring it in line with US requirements. For further information contact the Department of Transportation (**www.dot.gov**).

You will find that cars are relatively cheap in the United States (certainly considerably less expensive than in the UK). Should you leave Florida to return home, you may well consider taking your car with you.

Hiring a vehicle

Car rentals are much cheaper than in the UK. The main drawback, however, is that the level of insurance included in the quoted price is totally inadequate, and you may find yourself bankrupt if you cause an injury to a third party and have not taken out extra cover. Any cover under $1 million will expose you to a significant risk. You should take a look at exactly what cover is included in the hire, and the options for extending cover. Generally the minimum age for hiring a car is 21, though some rental companies insist on 25. In any event, those under 25 pay an additional charge. Your UK or Canadian licence will suffice, but an international driving permit will not.

Vehicle registration and driving licences

You are required to register your vehicle and obtain Florida licence plates for your vehicle(s) within 10 days of establishing residency, or of obtaining employment, or of a child's enrolment in school in Florida. The registration fee is $100, and there are further fees for the plate and a title charge. You must replace your metal plates every five years. This is because the reflective properties of the plate deteriorate with time. Plates are personal to you, and must be changed when ownership of a vehicle changes. Registration is renewed annually, but on the birthday of the registered owner. The registration (or an official copy) must be kept in the vehicle at all times, and can be asked for by a police officer. You will need Florida insurance in order to register your vehicle. The minimum coverage is $10,000 personal injury protection (PIP) and $10,000 property damage liability (PDL), although those who have been involved in a crash or have committed certain offences can be required to take out coverage for bodily injury liability (BIL).

UK registration documents should be returned to the DVLA, from whom a Certificate of Permanent Export (V561) should be obtained.

Motorboats and sailboats used in Florida waters for 90 days or more must be registered in Florida.

You have 30 days following establishing your residency in which to obtain a Florida driver's licence. You become resident immediately you enrol your child in a public school, accept employment or register to vote, or have been resident in Florida for more than six consecutive months. Any non-resident attending college in Florida is exempt. Applicants for a licence are required to undergo eyesight and hearing tests and two written exams (multi-choice questions on driving law and road signs), even if you already have a licence, even from another state of the United States. You will need two forms of identification to establish your date of birth.

Non-residents may apply for a 'Florida only' licence. This will entitle them to retain their foreign driving licence.

Insurance

There are a number of differences between the regulations in the UK and Florida governing motor insurance. A major difference is that whilst third-party liability insurance is compulsory, the minimum levels of compulsory cover (see above) are totally inadequate. You must obtain a higher level – failure to do so could result in your bankruptcy should you injure someone and be found even partially at fault. $1 million would be a minimum, but even this may not cover the costs of a claim against you by a person or persons who have sustained very serious injuries.

Florida does, however, have no-fault insurance. This means that if you are injured in an accident you do not have to bring a claim against the other driver, and prove that he was at fault. You simply claim against your own policy which pays out irrespective of who was at fault. Here again, however, the minimum level of cover is very limited – $10,000 for bodily injury and the same for damage to property.

The cost of insurance in the United States is high, though you do not generally pay a very large additional premium for a second or subsequent vehicle.

You should ensure that you fully understand the extent of the cover under any policy you are contemplating taking out. Take care also that you comply with the conditions contained in the policy, including the time limits and other provisions for the reporting of claims.

Car crime

In Florida car crime is a major problem. Ensure that your insurance policy is wide enough to include all valuable contents. Do not park your car (even for a few minutes) in an unsafe area, and do not help the car thief by leaving the original registration papers in the car. Always (discreetly) place valuables in the boot if you have to leave them in the car. You should report the theft of your vehicle to the police station nearest to the place from where it was stolen. You will need to go in person. If you are unable to attend immediately, telephone and go later.

Driving regulations

Drivers and front seat passengers must wear seat belts. Children must wear seat belts, including in the rear. Children between the ages of four and six years old may wear seat belts or an approved restraint seat. An approved child restraint seat is obligatory for infants and children under four. The driver is responsible for any breach and can be fined up to $500.

It is illegal to carry an open container of an alcoholic drink in a vehicle. One of the most striking differences between Florida and the UK is the speed at which people drive – in Florida the speed limit is rather lower than in the UK. The limit on interstate highways in Florida is 70 mph and 60 mph on most other highways, but speeds on urban roads can be as low as 15 mph, for example in school zones at certain times of the day. Radar detectors are used in Florida. Other major differences include the fact that drivers frequently overtake on either side, and the high priority that must be given to school buses (generally yellow). You should stop at least 25 feet behind a school bus that is taking on or discharging passengers. You should *never* pass a school bus that has its red lights flashing. Punishments for breach of the priority rules for school buses are severe, and can include community service, or in serious cases imprisonment. It is illegal to drive with a blood-alcohol level of 35 micrograms of alcohol per 100 ml.

For further information in relation to regulations governing vehicles and driving see **www.fhp.state.fl.us**, the website of Florida Highway Patrol. Indeed, motorists are advised to obtain a (free) copy of *The Florida Driver's Handbook* from the Florida Department of Highway Safety and Motor Vehicles (**www.hsmv.state.fl.us**). Information can also be obtained from the American Automobile Association, tel: (407) 894 3333, **www.aaasouth.com**. It is worthwhile considering joining the AAA as it provides a range of benefits to members.

For a list of garages that can repair British vehicles see **www.sunnybrits.com** (go to 'resources' then 'auto repair shops').

The Florida Sun Pass

This is a pre-paid toll system that is being applied by the Florida Department of Transportation to most of Florida's toll roads. It reduces congestion, and saves drivers' time and expense. Users receive a small pocket-sized 'transponder' which attaches to the inside of the windscreen.

As a vehicle passes through the toll lane the toll charge is automatically deducted from your pre-paid account. The transponder costs the motorist $25. He or she must also pay a minimum of $25 into the pre-paid account. Motorists using the system 40 or more times in a calendar month on those roads included in the scheme receive a rebate of 10 per cent. When the motorist's prepaid account balance is low the transponder emits a series of tones and a yellow light appears. Balances can be checked on the Sun Pass website **www.SunPass.com**. Transponders can be ordered online or by telephoning the SunPass Customer Service Center on 1 (888) 865 5352.

Disabled parking permits

You will need form HSMV 83039 which must be signed by a doctor. Information about parking permits can be obtained by telephoning the Customer Service Center on (850) 922 9000.

Accidents

Always report an accident to the law enforcement agency in order that a law enforcement officer can complete a report. Do not enter into negotiations with the other driver. Notify your own insurance company as soon as possible, and tell them if you believe that the other driver was uninsured.

Florida's Lemon Law

The Motor Vehicle Warranty Enforcement Act (commonly referred to as Florida's Lemon Law) provides purchasers of new motor vehicles with a certain degree of protection, and makes manufacturers responsible for replacing defective vehicles or refunding a customer's outlay. It applies to all new or demonstrator motor vehicles sold or leased in Florida, and to defects or conditions that substantially impair the use, value or safety of the vehicle. It does not apply (with some exceptions) to used vehicles, or minor defects. The Lemon Law created arbitration boards throughout Florida which decide complaints between purchasers and car manufacturers.

To bring a claim under the Lemon Law you must have taken the vehicle to the dealership or authorized agent at least three times for the same substantial defect or condition, or the vehicle must have been off the road for at least 15 consecutive days due to one or more substantial defects or conditions. You can then submit your Motor Vehicle Defect Notification Form to the manufacturer. You will find the form in the *Lemon Law Handbook* which should be given to you when you purchase a vehicle. This gives the manufacturer a right to carry out a final repair or inspection of your vehicle. Further information, including time limits, can be obtained from the Florida Attorney General's Office or by telephoning the Division of Consumer Services on 1 (800) 321 5366 or (850) 410 3807. Some vehicle manufacturers have their own arbitration programme, and if their programme has been approved by the state of Florida then you may be required to complain using that procedure first.

The New Motor Vehicle Arbitration Board will normally hear your claim within 40 days of accepting your request, and give its judgment within a further 60 days. The Board has the power to require the manufacturer to refund the purchase price plus certain expenses or to replace the vehicle. The consumer will have to pay a reasonable charge for the use that he or she has had of the original vehicle. There is a right of appeal from the Arbitration Board to a court. If a manufacturer appeals in bad faith, the judge has the power to double or triple the damages payable.

Buying second-hand cars

It is advisable to obtain a history report on any second-hand car that you are contemplating buying. Companies offering such reports include Carfax (**www.carfax.com**) and Experian Automotive. The Florida Department of Highway Safety and Motor Vehicles keeps details relating to salvage vehicles, including those damaged in recent hurricanes (see below for the web address).

Useful information

To find distances between locations go to www.myflorida.com – visitor – travelling to Florida – Highways and Roads

The Department of Highway Safety and Motor Vehicles website is **www.hsmv.state.fl.us/offices** where you will find much information, including a list of local offices.

10 Letting and selling your Florida home

A very high proportion of people who buy a property in Florida, other than as a principal residence, intend to rent out their property. Some will have purchased purely as an investment; others will want to reside in the property for shorter or longer periods of time (up to a maximum of six months per year for non-residents) but hope to partially offset the costs of a property by renting it out. In either case, purchasers should bear in mind that it is most unlikely that they will meet all their costs, including mortgage payments, from the rental income. It is illegal in Florida for agents to give guarantees of rental income, and estimates should also be treated with extreme caution.

Holiday lettings

If you intend to spend only short periods in your property, you could consider trying to let it out to other holiday visitors during the holiday seasons. Florida remains a top destination for tourists. In the south especially, and in the all-year-round tourist areas such as Orlando, the holiday letting season can last many months of the year. In the most popular resorts there is a strong demand for both holiday and longer-term lettings. The location of the property is obviously important for its letting potential. It should also have the basic facilities. Air-conditioning is really essential throughout Florida.

Even if you intend to live in the property more or less continuously, you may still wish to consider letting for short periods. In much of the south of Florida, it should be possible to let a home on a holiday rental during much of the year, at a rental income rather higher than the monthly mortgage instalments.

Many foreign Florida property owners manage lettings themselves, placing advertisements on a number of internet sites or in newspapers and magazines in the UK or Canada or, indeed, in Florida. With over 1 million British tourists visiting Florida each year, and a similarly large number of Canadians, you should have no problem finding holiday tenants. If you work in a large organization, such as a local authority, hospital or private company, or have a good friend who does, you may be able to circulate details among the employees. Your own small internet site (at a modest cost of about £400) is also worth considering. Professional-looking photographs are imperative, as is a rental agreement drawn up by a local attorney.

You should note that in many counties and cities there are significant local government restrictions on short-term lettings (such as a ban on lettings under 30 days), and that there are also restrictions in many blocks of flats or residential developments as to the renting out of dwellings. It is imperative that you ascertain the position before making any assumptions about the letting potential of a property that you intend to purchase. Not only can county and city rules change, but the other property owners in a residential development could decide to vote in a change of rules relating to the letting of dwellings in the development, thereby severely restricting your ability to let.

Properties that are let out must be licensed with the state of Florida and with the county authority. You should establish contact with the Florida State Division of Hotels and Restaurants from whom you will need a licence that must be displayed on the premises. You must ascertain from the local county hall what their requirements are for compliance with fire and safety regulations. Your property will be subject to inspections to check on compliance.

Those letting property are required to charge sales tax of between 6 and 7.5 per cent, depending on the county, on all rentals of less than six months, even if the rent is paid to you outside of the United States. There are additional tourist development taxes in most counties, bringing the total tax you must charge on rentals up to about 11 per cent. Prior to letting the property you must lodge an Application for Sales and Use Tax Registration with the Florida Department of Revenue. You will have to submit a monthly sales tax return and account for the tax you have received.

If you are not going to be around when your property is being let, remember that you will need someone who can arrange to have the property cleaned for you, deal with handovers and any emergencies that may arise. Ideally, you should also have that person place some basic supplies, such as fresh bread, butter, milk and mineral water, in the property in preparation for the arrival of your guests.

Alternatively, you can instruct one of a number of Florida management agents. Management agents charge a hefty commission (generally around 15 per cent of gross rental income), and further fees for any services provided. The latter include cleaning and maintenance, but also a 'meet and greet' service to welcome your clients. Management agencies vary tremendously in the quality of the service they provide. You will need to keep a close eye on them to ensure that they are keeping the property as fully let as possible, and are providing a good service to your clients (especially with regard to keeping the property clean). Insist on being provided with a week-by-week schedule of rental income with contact details of tenants – some agencies have been known to keep part of the rental income for themselves during peak periods or to fail to inform proprietors of a letting during the low season. If you know someone who lives nearby who can make spot checks, so much the better. You should insist that the rental income is placed in an escrow account and paid to you on a regular basis to reduce your losses should the agency fold.

The return that you can expect from renting out your Florida property will depend on a number of factors, not least the effort that you put into finding clients, the location of the property, accessibility from the UK and Canada, and the attractiveness of the property. You should prepare a brief information pack. Of crucial importance are good directions to the property – if these are complicated, then potential clients may be put off. In your description of the area, you should include references to the main tourist attractions, particularly those in close proximity to the property, as well as local restaurants, supermarkets, banks, markets, pharmacies, doctors and hospitals. A good map showing the property, main landmarks and attractions is essential. The best bookings are from clients who wish to return.

Longer-term lettings

Before letting out your property on a longer-term letting, I recommend that you read Chapter 3, which sets out the main considerations in detail, albeit from a tenant's perspective. Tenants have fewer rights than in the UK, and far fewer than elsewhere in western Europe.

You can take a security deposit (usually one month's rent, but it can be higher). The deposit is paid as a guarantee of the condition of the property and the other risks taken by the proprietor in letting the property. At the end of the rental, the deposit is returned to the tenant, less your costs of rectifying any damage to the property and any unpaid rent (see Chapter 3 for your obligations in relation to the deposit).

Before a tenant moves in, you should arrange to draw up a document setting out the condition of the property (again, see Chapter 3, and the checklist included in that chapter), and have the tenant sign an inventory of the items included in the rental.

As a landlord, you are responsible for maintaining the structure of the building, including the roof and boundaries, stairs, shutters and windows, boiler and chimney. The tenant is responsible for running repairs, such as minor works of maintenance to prevent the building falling into disrepair – tasks such as painting, replacing windowpanes, cleaning and minor repairs to pipework, taps and radiators, replacing the odd broken floor tile.

The nightmare tenant

Whether you are letting your property for short-term holiday lets or for longer periods, there is always the risk of encountering a tenant who will not leave or does so only after causing extensive damage to your property. You can take out insurance against such eventualities. There are various policies available with different levels of cover.

Insurance

You should make your insurers aware that you are letting the property and the type of lettings involved. Failure to do so may result in a claim being disallowed. You must also take out public liability insurance to protect you against any claims by clients or other visitors to the property.

Income tax on income from Florida property

Income tax is payable if you let your property for more than 14 days in any one year. Non-residents are taxed at a rate of 30 per cent of the gross rental income unless they opt to pay tax on a net basis. The latter option permits proprietors to deduct a variety of expenses, including mortgage interest and property taxes, which often results in a nil net income and hence no liability to tax. Furthermore, losses can be carried forward, and any net profit is taxed at only 15 per cent. In order to exercise this option, non-residents must first have a US identification number, usually obtainable from the local social security office.

All owners of property are required to submit a tax return, even if they derive no income from their property. The deadline is 15 June each year, and most non-residents arrange for this to be completed by a financial adviser such as an accountant, or their management company. The option for assessment on a net basis is exercised when completing your tax form 1040 NR. You must also complete a form 4224. Those jointly owning property must each complete their own separate forms declaring half the gross income and setting off half the deductible expenses. If you do not properly opt for the net basis then the management agency is required to retain 30 per cent of the gross rental income.

You may also be liable to pay income tax on the rental income in your home country, although any tax you have paid in the United States should be taken into account under the relevant double taxation treaty.

Selling your property

Whilst a large number of vendors do sell their property themselves, most homes in Florida are sold via agents. An agent is required to obtain a written authorization from the vendor or his or her legal representative. You can choose between entering into a multiple listing service (MLS) or an exclusive contract. With the former, the broker you have appointed will pass details of your property to all other dealers taking part in the MLS. Your broker will then share the commission with whichever agent locates a buyer. With an exclusive contract the agent has the sole right to find a buyer, though you will generally pay a lower commission than if you opt for an MLS.

Real estate agents generally demand a commission of between 5 and 7 per cent of the sale price, although you may succeed in agreeing a lower rate if the market is buoyant and the agent is confident of locating a purchaser reasonably quickly. If there is any prospect of your finding a buyer yourself you should insist that the agreement allows you to do this without becoming liable for the agent's commission – failure to do this will render you liable to pay his or her commission in full. One possibility is to agree that in the event of your finding a purchaser the agent should receive only a proportion of the agreed commission.

For those wishing to sell their Florida home themselves, there are numerous publications and websites, both in the UK and Canada and in Florida itself, where you can advertise your property. Obviously, professional-looking photographs are essential.

In most states in the US the law requires vendors to disclose defects or problems with their property, and imposes penalties on those who fraudulently conceal substantial defects. More and more states are passing such laws, and many states have disclosure forms that vendors are required to complete. Increasingly states that have had such laws for some time are adding to or strengthening these requirements. Accordingly you should obtain up-to-date advice from a Florida real estate lawyer as to your legal obligations. Usually you will only need to provide details of problems within your personal knowledge, or which should have been obvious to you. Often a vendor will instruct a building contractor to take a look at the property to advise on what should be disclosed. He or she will frequently be able to provide you with a valuation of the property, and/or an estimate of the cost of any works of repair that are required, which may speed up your negotiations with prospective purchasers.

Your lawyer should ensure that the purchaser acknowledges receipt of the disclosures. He or she should also be able to advise you of any local provisions for disclosure that affect your property.

For those selling a house that was constructed before 1978, you are required to disclose the presence of any lead-based paint and to inform any purchaser of the hazards associated with lead-based paints. The Residential Lead-Based Paint Hazard Reduction Act 1992 provides that vendors should supply buyers with an explanatory leaflet produced by the US Environmental Protection Agency. It also states that the contract should include various warnings and confirm that the regulations have been followed, and that purchasers should have a ten-day opportunity for testing the house for lead. Failure to comply with these requirements can enable the buyer to claim substantial damages against you. Further information is available from the Agency's website **www.epa.gov** (go to 'lead').

Capital gains tax (see Chapter 14) is payable on the increase in value of the property on a sale. In the case of non-residents an agent is required to retain 10 per cent of the sale price as a guarantee of the ultimate payment of any capital gains tax liability. At the end of the tax year the non-resident must submit form 1040 NR on which he or she records the capital gain. US residents complete form 2119 to file with their 1040 tax form.

11 Education and health

Those wishing to place their children in a publicly funded school need to prove residency, that is, in practice, be in possession of a visa permitting them to work. In addition to public schools, there are also many good private schools. A good source of information about all educational matters, and activities for children, covering south Florida is **www.southflorida.com/sfparenting** (the publishers of *South Florida Parenting Magazine*).

The standard of public education in Florida varies considerably, with wealthier areas generally receiving more funding, and the students obtaining higher results. In the 1990s education campaigners brought a challenge before the courts in an attempt to challenge the basis of funding public schools. They lost, but in 1998 succeeded in having an amendment passed to the state constitution that substantially strengthened the state's obligations to educate its children. The addition to the constitution reads as follows:

> *The education of children is a fundamental value of the people of the State of Florida. It is, therefore, a paramount duty of the state to make adequate provision for the education of all children residing within its borders. Adequate provision shall be made by law for a uniform, efficient, safe, secure, and high quality system of free public schools that allows students to obtain a high quality education...*

In 2002 the constitution was again amended to provide that class sizes in core-curriculum courses should be reduced by two students each year from 2003/4 onwards, so that by the beginning of the 2010/11 school year they would fall to 18 for pre-kindergarten to grade 3, 22 pupils for grades 4 to 8, and 25 pupils for grades 9 to 12.

The Florida A-Plus choice and accountability system was also introduced to force schools to improve their academic performance. Under this scheme, every public school in Florida was assigned a grade (A–F) according to its results in the Florida Comprehensive Assessment Test. Students in schools that received two F grades in four years were entitled to vouchers that permitted them to transfer to a private school or another public school. The results indicate that schools that received an F in 1999 were able to improve their results significantly for the following year, to avoid the consequences of a second failed result! The lesson taken from the scheme was that when public schools faced the risk that their students might receive vouchers and leave the school, they improved their performance.

In 1999 the Governor of Florida established the Florida Mentoring Partnership. This programme has succeeded in its original aim to recruit 200,000 volunteers to act as mentors to children of school age. Experience has demonstrated that students with mentors perform better at school and have higher rates of moving on to third-level education compared to non-mentored students. Studies show dramatic falls in illegal drug use and school absenteeism. For further information see: **www.flcities.com/mentoring/**.

Over the past six years or so, the public education system has undergone a number of other important developments, some of which I summarize below.

Public schools in Florida are administered on the basis of each county. You can locate a public or private school (or pre-school) in any given city or county on the site **www.floridasmart.com** by going to education and then Florida schools. You can find out information about the performance and standards of public schools over the previous five years by searching the website of the Florida School Indicators Report: **www.info.doe.state.fl.us/fsir**.

Pre-school education

September 2005 sees the opening of Florida's Voluntary Universal Pre-Kindergarten Program. This is a voluntary programme for four-year-olds, and provides a three- or six-hour day of pre-school for children who are eligible to begin kindergarten the following school year (Year 1 Infants in the UK – see table 11.1). Numerous institutions are participating within both the public and private sectors, and include childcare centres as well as schools. Further information about the programme and in relation to kindergartens, including lists for each county, can be found on the site **www.floridasmart.com**.

Just Read, Florida

This is a state-wide programme set up in 2001 to substantially raise the level of reading amongst Florida's school children. It is primarily aimed at those in public schools. It is founded on educational research, and makes use of phonic-based teaching methods (ie, where the child learns the link between sounds and letters) and comprehension. For more information see **www.justreadflorida.com.**

Choices for primary and secondary education

State schools

As with all types of school, standards in state schools vary considerably. In some areas, the presence of significant numbers of non-native English speakers is putting a considerable strain on school resources. A fairly recent innovation to improve the management and financing of schools is the *Charter School*. Charter schools are often referred to as 'independent public schools'. These schools are operated by non-profit-making associations, generally run by a combination of parents, teachers, local councils and/or universities. They are funded primarily by the Florida Department of Education on the same basis as other public schools, but they obtain additional funding via grants and private donations. They are non-fee-paying. Any child living in the school district in which the school is situated may attend the school. If there are insufficient places for the number of applications, then students are selected on a random basis.

Other developments include *commuter schools* and *satellite schools*. Both are public schools. Commuter schools are schools that children attend near one or other of their parents' place of work, rather than the nearest school to their home. A satellite school is a school that operates on the premises of a large employer, with the staff and equipment being provided by the state.

Private Florida schools

There is a wide range of private schools in Florida. You can find information and assistance in selecting private schools at **www.nais.org**, the website of the National Association of Independent Schools, and also from the Florida Council of Independent Schools (**www.fcis.org**) and the

Southern Association of Colleges and Schools (**www.sacs.org**). You will also find helpful information and articles in *South Florida Parents Magazine.*

Internet (school) education

There are two online schools in Florida, the University of Miami On Line High School and the Florida Virtual School (**www.flvs.net**), offering teaching for children from grades 8 to 12. Both schools have been officially accredited by the Southern Association of Colleges and Schools (SACS) and the Commission on International and Trans-Regional Education. They now provide a service to students throughout the United States and in the wider world. The Miami On Line High School provides qualified teaching staff, claims to be flexible, and states that courses are personalized to meet individual student needs. Major advantages are that a student can start a course at any time, and can work entirely at their own pace. Students cannot be held back by their class, nor can they fall behind the class. The courses are particularly suited to children who are unable to attend school regularly, such as young athletes and performers, or those living abroad, and also those educated at home. However, students do not have to enrol for the entire high school diploma – those attending a traditional school can enrol simply to add to the credits they will obtain at their school. Parents can access their child's progress reports. The Miami On Line High School offers summer school courses lasting ten weeks and starting at any time between 1 May and 15 July. The cost is $500 per course, but enables you and your child to try out and evaluate the course and its teaching methods before making a more substantial commitment.

The Florida Virtual School, established in 1997 and funded by the state of Florida on a similar basis to more traditional public schools, now has more than 20,000 students (including adults). It also provides training to other teachers, and administrators, in other parts of the United States on how to deliver online tuition. The school can be contacted on (407) 317 3326.

Homeschooling

For detailed information on this subject see the website of the Florida Parent Educators Association **www.fpea.com** and their guide to home-schooling in Florida, and also the above section on virtual schools.

Child protection

You can check whether anyone who has or might have care of your children has a conviction for a sex offence or other crime by consulting the website **www.childcarechecker.com**. There is a charge of $10 for this service.

Table 11.1 Equivalent stages of education for the United Kingdom and the United States

AGE	UK	UNITED STATES
2–5	NURSERY	NURSERY
5–6	INFANT	
	Yr 1 (infants)	KINDERGARTEN
		ELEMENTARY
6–7	Yr 2 (infants)	1st grade
7–8	Yr 3 (junior)	2nd grade
8–9	Yr 4 (junior)	3rd grade
9–10	Yr 5 (junior)	4th grade
10–11	Yr 6 (junior)	5th grade
11–12	1st form	6th grade
		JUNIOR HIGH
12–13	2nd form	7th grade
13–14	3rd form	8th grade
		HIGH SCHOOL
14–15	4th form	9th grade
15–16	5th form	10th grade
16–17	Lower 6th	11th grade
17–18	Upper 6th	12th grade

University and third-level education

There are 10 public universities in Florida (for a list see **www. floridasmart.com** – education – colleges and universities), and a large selection of independent colleges and universities. There are also 28 community colleges.

The Open University

The Open University's distance learning programme is available in the United States, though the range of courses available is somewhat limited. Information about the Open University's courses and the Open University Business School can be found on their respective websites: **www.open.ac.uk** and **www.oubs.open.ac.uk**. A list of courses available in the United States can be seen at **www.3.open.ac.uk/courses/ countries/usa.shtm**.

Useful educational websites

Florida Department of Education: **www.fldoe.org**
Florida Association of Christian Schools and Colleges: **www.faccs.org**
Florida Distance Learning Consortium: **www.distancelearn.org**
Florida School Indicators Report (FSIR): **www.info.doe.state.fl.us/fsir/**
Florida Education Association: **www.feaweb.org** (has many links to national and state sites, public schools, 213 South Adams Street, Tallahassee, FL 32301, tel: (850) 201 2800)
Florida Education Channel (TV): **www.fec.tv**
Florida Parent Educators Association: **www.fpea.com**
Broward County Schools: **www.browardschools.com**; Palm Beach County Schools: **www.palmbeach.k12.fl.us**; Miami-Dade County Schools: **www.dadeschools.net**
www.virtualsage.org – online tuition
www.upkflorida.org; **www.floridajobs.org/earlylearning**;
www.teachinflorida.com; **www.justreadflorida.com**;
www.justsciencenow.com
www.BBCAmericashop.com; **www.collegesurfing.com**

Healthcare and the US health system

The United States does not have a national health system, apart from Medicare, which is limited to those aged over 65 and the disabled, and Medicaid which is restricted to the very poor. To be entitled to that assistance from Medicare, however, you would have to have worked for a substantial period in the United States. Whilst there is an agreement between the United States and the UK that allows contributions to the UK system to be counted for qualifying for other state benefits, the agreement does not extend to hospital cover. For further details in relation to Medicare see its website at **www.medicare.gov**.

In practice, expatriates require private health insurance. You need a high level of cover, and should regard $1 million as a minimum. The cover should include hospital treatment. Consider whether you need to include repatriation to your home country. Expect cover to be expensive, and you should shop around. Premiums of $1,000 to $1,500 for a family *per month* are common. The larger insurers include Blue Cross, Blue Shield and Major Medical. The cost will be determined in large part by your age and pre-existing conditions. Higher premiums are common not only for smokers, but also for those who are overweight. You can reduce your premiums by agreeing to a higher deductible (ie the amount that you have to pay towards your medical bills before your insurance 'kicks in'). Note that most standard policies do not cover pre-existing conditions or include maternity cover, baby care and dental treatment, opticians' charges, intensive care and care for the terminally ill, and you will need to consider the various add-on options.

You may be able to obtain less expensive cover through a professional organization, which will normally have a group policy. Take a look at the website of the Agency for Healthcare Research and Quality, **www.ahcpr.gov**, which provides general advice on heath insurance. Remember that all applicants for health cover owe a duty to fully disclose pre-existing conditions. If you do not, and the insurance company later finds out that you have not been frank, you could face a claim being disallowed. You can also obtain a guide to health insurance published by the Florida Department of Insurance, tel: (850) 413 3100. Ensure that you read *all* the small print on the policy document before entering into the insurance contract.

You may find that US insurance companies are reluctant to give you cover, or will do so only on payment of very high premiums, because they consider that they have inadequate details of your medical history. There are, however, a number of European companies that specialize in providing expatriates with health insurance.

Note that Britons living abroad who return on a temporary visit to the UK are required to pay privately for all treatment, except emergency treatment.

In the United States most health cover is paid wholly or more usually only partially by employers, as part of the employees' remuneration package. Employers take out a group plan for which no individual medical examination is required, but frequently this does not extend to spouses and children. The level of cover provided varies from the fully comprehensive to the extremely basic. A high proportion of Florida residents, however, have no cover at all, or cover that is wholly insufficient. Increasingly employers are requiring employees to share a greater proportion of the health insurance burden, the employee contributions being deducted from the salary paid by the employer.

One option worth considering is taking out one of the policies available via the Florida Association of British Business. It apparently offers reasonably priced cover backed by Lloyds through Mainstream Insurance, tel: (561) 392 4485. Apparently applicants must hold a British passport and a US work visa. Details of health insurance can also be obtained from a search of 'health insurance' on **www.iprowl.com**. It may also be worth consulting the Independent Healthcare Association, 22 Little Russell Street, London WC1A 2HT, tel: 0207 430 0537.

The cost of health insurance has caused considerable concern across the United States. In 2003 the Governor of Florida set up a task force to consider steps to improve the provision of health care in Florida, and in particular to reduce the cost of cover. A number of steps have been carried out (see Chapter 13), and further encouragement has been given to the Health Savings Accounts that enable small employers to join together to purchase health care cover at more economical rates. See **www.fldfs.com/consumers** for a list of companies that will provide health insurance to small companies.

Health cover for Canadians

All Canadian provinces provide only very limited coverage for Canadians abroad, and they will pay only a small proportion of the cost of US health care. Those who visit Florida for prolonged periods take out special insurance. This costs in the region of $750 for a 90-day period for persons over 65. A further complication for Canadians is that their public health coverage lapses completely after six months spent away, and it can take around three months to re-qualify.

Vaccinations

You are likely to be required to give details of vaccinations to your doctor, or your children's doctor, and indeed as a condition of school entry.

12 Immigration into the United States

Whilst there are no restrictions on foreigners buying property in Florida, or elsewhere in the United States, most foreigners are not allowed to remain in the United States for more than three months, unless they have a residence permit (the 'green card') or a visa. Visitors must also be in possession of a passport that will remain valid for at least six months after the end of their trip to the United States.

The United States welcomes over 800,000 lawful immigrants each year, with Florida being one of the most popular destinations for new arrivals. Over half of these immigrants rely on a marriage or family connection. The balance includes about 140,000 employment-based immigrants, around 120,000 refugees, and 55,000 winners of the diversity lottery (see below). In addition there are a sizeable number of illegal immigrants. Many of these have crossed over from Mexico or Canada, but a larger number consists of those who have legitimately entered the United States on student, tourist or business visas but have not returned to their home country.

The procedure for immigrating to the United States is long and bureaucratic. It was administered by the Immigration and Naturalization Service (INS), but this is now known as the Bureau of Citizenship and Immigration Services (BCIS) and comes under the auspices of the Office of Homeland Security. Whilst you will find more detailed information in books specializing on this subject, and on various internet sites, you should seriously consider consulting an experienced immigration attorney who, often for a fixed fee of around $300, will provide you with preliminary advice on the best route to take, and your prospects of success. It is also advisable to instruct an attorney to file the papers on your behalf, as it is very easy for those unfamiliar with the system to make an unnecessary error that results in the application being refused, or delayed. A lawyer's services for this can be expensive, depending on the complexities involved in your application, and the time taken to prepare it.

Those entering the United States are classified as either non-immigrants (temporary residents) or immigrants (those wishing to settle permanently in the United States).

Immigrants

Immigrants are entitled to work permanently in the United States, and qualify for US citizenship after five years. The categories of immigrants include:

▋ the spouse, child, parent, widow or widower of a US citizen;
▋ other family members of US citizens;
▋ foreigners with outstanding abilities or skills, or investors with generally at least $1 million capital and who will be employing 10 or more US persons;
▋ religious workers;
▋ employees of the United States abroad;
▋ diversity lottery immigrants (see below);
▋ refugees from persecution.

Immediate relatives

The spouse, child, parent, widow or widower of a US citizen is entitled, as of right, to an immigrant visa. There is no limit on the number of those entitled to a visa on this ground.

Family-based immigration

Those entitled to apply consist of: the unmarried son or daughter over 21 of a US citizen, the spouse or unmarried son or daughter of a lawful permanent resident, the brother or sister of a US citizen over 21, and the married son or daughter of a US citizen. There is an annual quota for visas in this category (of around 200,000) and applicants often have to wait several years before they are successful.

Employment-based immigration (EB)

Usually, successful applicants must have a specific offer of employment from an employer based in the United States. There is an annual quota, and five subcategories that take up the quota in order of preference, with most applicants falling into the first three categories. Priority is firstly given to those with exceptional ability in the sciences, education, the arts or sport, outstanding professors and researchers, and some multinational executives and managers. In the second category are professionals with advanced degrees and workers with exceptional ability in the sciences, arts or business. The third category covers professionals, skilled and unskilled workers. Employers sponsoring applicants in the second and third category must satisfy the Department of Labor that the position cannot be filled with a US worker. The Labor Certification process is notoriously slow.

The Diversity/Green Card Lottery

Every year the United States makes available 55,000 'diversity' visas to natives of foreign countries from which immigration in the previous five years was less than 50,000 people (Section 131 of the Immigration Act 1990). Applicants from such countries must have been educated to at least high school level, or have worked for at least two of the previous five years in an occupation that requires two years or more of training or experience. The UK is not a low admission country, but Ireland is (and this includes Northern Ireland). You do not have to be resident in your native country at the time of application, and accordingly UK residents who were born in Ireland or Northern Ireland may apply. The spouse of a native of a 'low admission' country is also entitled to apply. Those eligible to enter the lottery may do so in addition to submitting any visa application, and may make repeated applications each year.

Dates for submitting lottery applications change, and you should check with the Department of State, which is responsible for administering the lottery, not the BCIS. The website is **www.travel.state.gov**. No fee is charged, and there is no application form. Entrants simply type basic details on a blank piece of paper, and send this together with a recent photograph to the DV Program at the National Visa Center in Portsmouth NH. The zip code varies depending on the geographical region from which you are applying. You should check the above website for up-to-date details.

Non-immigrants

Those with a non-immigrant visa are permitted to enter and to stay in the United States for a limited period of time, and for limited purposes. No separate work permit is required – those permitted to work will have this recorded on their visa. These visas are: Government Officials (A), Visitor (B-1, B-2),Transit (C), Crew (D), Treaty Trader or Investor (E-1, E-2), Academic Student (F), International Organization Representative (G), Speciality Occupation Workers (H-1B, these include in particular nurses, and those providing services that are not available in the United States), Temporary Workers (H-2B), Foreign Press (I), Student/Teacher Exchange (J), Fiancée/Fiancé (K), Intracompany Transferees (L-1), Non-Academic Student (M), Parent/Child/Sibling of alien granted special immigrant status (N), aliens of Extraordinary Ability (O), Athletes/Entertainers (P); Cultural Exchange (Q); Religious Workers (R); Professional – Canadian/Mexican NAFTA (TN). Up-to-date information about visas can be obtained from and via the website of the US Embassy in London, **www.usembassy.org.uk**.

When entering or re-entering the United States, those in possession of a non-immigrant visa should carry proof of their entitlement with them (eg possession of sufficient funds to support themselves; a return ticket; evidence of the purpose of their trip), as immigration officials are not obliged to accept the visa at face value but may investigate whether you are lawfully qualified to enter the United States. Note that all children entering the United States must have their own passport, and cannot be included on a parent's passport.

It can take up to two months for a visa application to be processed, although in many cases applicants receive their visas within a month of lodging their application.

The B visas

Unless a native from a country covered by the visa waiver scheme, travellers to the United States on holiday must apply for a B-2 visa. The application form can be downloaded from **www.travel.state.gov**. Go to DS-156.pdf. Business travellers not covered by the visa waiver scheme should apply for a B-1 visa.

Visa waivers

Nationals of certain countries can visit the United States under a visa waiver scheme. The countries covered include the UK, Ireland, Australia,

New Zealand, all the Scandinavian countries, the Netherlands, most other EU countries and Japan. You must be in possession of a valid passport, and a return or onward non-transferable ticket, though this latter provision does not apply if you arrive by land from Canada or Mexico. The trip must be for business or pleasure, and is limited to 90 days. Note that all those wishing to enter under the visa waiver scheme must have a machine-readable passport – the old blue UK passports are insufficient, and holders should obtain a visa or a new UK passport.

The E-2 visa

The E-2 visa enables individuals who make an investment in a US-based business, or who start up their own business in the United States, to stay in the United States. Whilst the individual will normally be granted a stay of two years, this can be extended, and in practice investors remain for the whole of the period during which their investment continues. The spouse, and children under 21, of such investors also have the right to stay in the United States and attend school. Furthermore, the investor's spouse is also permitted to work, though he or she must apply for a work authorization document from the local branch of the USCIS. Children are not entitled to work and can no longer rely on their parent's entitlement once they reach 21, and may therefore have to leave the United States. *Any* type of business is permitted. Whilst you can apply direct to the immigration authorities, it is advisable to apply through your local US embassy or consulate. The official responsible often has a considerable degree of discretion, and you should contact him or her *before* lodging your application. Ideally you should try to speak to the person concerned for an informal discussion.

An applicant must make a 'substantial investment' in the United States. You will see frequent mention of a figure of $100,000. This is only a guideline. US law has not fixed any minimum level. Whether an investment is sufficient to be determined as 'substantial' depends on the particular circumstances, and could be much less than this 'guideline'. The investment must be a substantial part of the particular business in question. In many sectors, especially in the service industry, it is possible to start a new business with far less than $100,000, perhaps even well under a half of that amount. What the authorities are looking for is for the investor to bring a benefit to the local economy, in particular in terms of employment of US workers. A business employing two or three employees (in addition to the investor and his family) will frequently be sufficient. So too may be a business supported with a well-argued business plan that does not employ anyone initially, but has good prospects of doing so within the first year, or even of engaging subcontractors. With some businesses it is easy to show that the business will need the labour of persons other than the investor and his or her immediate family – for example a restaurant. In some cases the authorities will allow investors a longer period for the envisaged employment of US citizens, though the limit would be five years.

If you are purchasing a business, it is usual to place the purchase price in an 'escrow account', with payment to the vendor to be conditional upon the approval of the purchaser's E-2 visa application. You are not required to make your investment before you receive confirmation that you have been granted an E-2 visa, but you must be able to demonstrate that you have the funds available.

The investor must be able to show that he or she has sufficient control over the business to be able to sufficiently influence its development. In practice this means at least 50 per cent ownership. Thus two foreigners could together purchase a business with each having a 50 per cent ownership and be able to apply for E-2 visas.

One British lawyer who has emigrated to Florida and in conjunction with a Florida Attorney offers advice on emigration to the US is Peter Gold (**www.emigrationtotheusa.com**).

The most commonly used working visas (E, H, L)

The H-1B Speciality Occupation Workers visa: this is for speciality occupation workers. This essentially covers professionals, such as accountants, lawyers, teachers, software specialists. A prospective employer will need to show that:

▪ the applicant has the equivalent of at least a bachelor's degree;
▪ the job is one that ordinarily requires the degree that the prospective employee has;
▪ the employer will pay the applicant at least the prevailing salary for that position.

The visa is initially valid for up to three years, and can be extended for a further three years. Spouses and children are granted H-4 visas but are not permitted to work.

The H-1C Registered Nurse visa: the United States grants a number of visas annually to those coming to provide nursing care in sectors in which there is a shortage.

The H-2 Temporary Worker visa: this enables employers to hire skilled or semi-skilled foreigners in posts for which the employer has a temporary need that cannot be met by appointing a US worker. The employer must first go through the Department of Labor to obtain a grant of a temporary labour certificate, once it has determined whether there are US workers that can fill the post. The visa is initially valid for 12 months. It can be extended for two further 12 month periods. Dependents are given an H-4 visa and may not work.

The L-1 Intracompany Transferee visa: this is a frequently used category and covers executives, managers, and those with specialized knowledge who are transferred to the United States *within* an international organization. To constitute an international organization, the parent company must have a branch office, subsidiary company, or affiliate company in the United States. The subsidiary or affiliate company must be at least 50 per cent owned by the foreign parent company. Accordingly, it is possible for those owning a foreign company to transfer themselves to the United States by setting up a branch office, or establishing a subsidiary or an affiliate in the United States. L-2 visas are given to family members who are not authorized to work.

The E-1 Treaty Traders and Investors visa: this covers investors and traders who wish to carry on their trade or business in the United States. The trade must be between the United States and the country of which the holder is a national, and the country must be one with which the US has a treaty.

The North American Free Trade Agreement (TN)

The above agreement provides for additional non-immigrant visa categories (TN) for citizens of Canada and Mexico. For the most part this covers only professional workers. Canadians may also apply for L-1 and H-1 visas at land border ports of entry and designated airports. You will need documentary evidence to prove eligibility. Entrants can work in the United States for up to one year, but can apply to renew annually. The arrangements are intended to enable Canadians to have their applications for visas processed quickly and with the minimum amount of paperwork. The speed at which applications are decided varies according to the border post. Once in the United States, TN status immigrants can apply for H, L or E status.

Taking American nationality

A person who is a lawful permanent resident is permitted to live and work in the United States indefinitely, and to sponsor certain family members for immigration. He or she must also pay US taxes. However, he or she is not a US citizen and cannot vote.

Those lawful permanent residents who have been *continuously* resident in the United States for at least five years after gaining the status of permanent resident are entitled to apply for naturalization. This can be reduced to three years for a person who has been married to and living with a US citizen for at least three years. There are a number of requirements, and applicants must check the up-to-date position. They include being of 'good moral character' (primarily not having a criminal conviction or having been involved in criminal activity), swearing an oath of allegiance, undergoing an English language test, and also a civics test to assess your knowledge of US history and government. Applicants must also attend a naturalization interview. Whilst the oath of allegiance involves renouncing all 'allegiance and fidelity' to any foreign state, the United States does permit its citizens and applicants for citizenship to have dual (or indeed multi-) nationality.

Before applying to become an American citizen (or indeed a citizen of any country) you should ensure that you are aware of both the advantages and the disadvantages. Your country of origin will not be prepared to interfere with any demands made upon you by your adopted country, such as military service, or indeed conscription. According to the Home Office, Her Majesty has no objection to British subjects applying for citizenship of a foreign state or states, without losing their British nationality. The Canadian and Irish governments take the same permissive stance.

Further information

Getting into America by Henry G Liebman (HowtoBooks)
How to become a US citizen by Debra R Shpigler (Thomson Learning)
How to get a job in America by Roger Jones (Howtobooks)
Bureau of Citizenship and Immigration Services (BCIS) website: **www.immigration.gov/graphics/howdoi/legpermres**

13 Working and setting up a business in Florida

Readers should first consult Chapter 12 on Immigration into the United States, given the restrictions on working placed on 'aliens'.

Employment

Florida has one of the best job creation programmes in the United States. For details visit the official website **www.myflorida.com**. Employ Florida Marketplace, **www.employflorida.com**, provides a job search facility, information on education and training and career assistance. This is said to be one of the most sophisticated sites that helps match employers and employees.

One-Stop Centers

This concept is designed for job seekers, students, employers and others associated with the employment market. Tools include precedents to assist in writing curricula vitae and correspondence with prospective employers; programmes to enable you to assess your own skills and training requirements, to improve your career prospects or change career; a notification service that alerts you to the posting of job offers corresponding to your skills; details of benefits for which you might be eligible; information as to current salary levels for particular job sectors.

You can also make contact with recruitment agencies by sending them a CV and covering letter requesting an appointment. Scan the classified ads in main newspapers, including the local British and Canadian press (notably for the British, the *Union Jack*, America's national monthly newspaper for Britons), and the various expatriate websites. Finally, it can be worth sending unsolicited well-written letters and CVs to companies you are interested in. A covering letter must always be hand-written and in perfect English. The CV should be very brief and to the point (one page only). The paper should be of good quality and the envelope should be white. Do not use A4 size paper but rather the standard US size which is 8.5″ × 11″.

Whilst there is no particular time that employers recruit, September and January are considered to be the best times to search for a new job. Consider using voice mail, and prepare a half-minute slot selling yourself. Foreign qualifications will not mean much to a US employer, so you should have your qualifications assessed, for example by Education International, 29 Denton Road, Wellesley, MA 02181.

Note that large British companies with a substantial presence in Florida employ local US workers, and do not recruit from amongst British citizens seeking work in Florida or seeking to move there. There are, however, many Britons and Canadians employed in businesses specializing in supplying a service to the British and Canadian communities in Florida, especially in the main population centres in the south of Florida. Many expatriates find employment opportunities by networking among fellow expatriates.

An ability to speak Spanish is obviously an advantage given the number of Florida residents of Hispanic origin, many of whom have a very poor command of English. There is also a very sizeable Canadian population (especially retired people who spend several months in Florida to avoid the bitter Canadian winter). Many of those from Quebec have only a limited knowledge of English, and accordingly there are openings for those with a high level of French in the various businesses run by and for French Canadians.

Teaching

For obvious reasons this is a huge employment sector. For a whole range of details about teaching, including jobs, see **www.teachinflorida.com**.

Nursing

Again this is a sector employing large numbers of people in Florida and there are frequently shortages and opportunities for foreigners. The United States grants temporary H-1C visas to a number of foreigners each year. You should begin by contacting:

The Commission on Graduates of Foreign Nursing Schools and the International Commission on Healthcare Professionals (CGFNS/ICHP)
3600 Market Street, Suite 400
Philadelphia, PA 19104–2651
Tel: (215) 349 8767; e-mail: info@cgfns.org.
Take a look at their website at: **www.cgfns.org**.

Tourism

Tourism is not surprisingly a major industry in Florida, and there is a huge demand for jobs in this sector. For the most part they are relatively poorly paid.

Jobs with the state government

Take a look at the website **www.peoplefirst.myflorida.com/logon.htm** where you will find details of employment in the public sector in Florida.

Job search websites

www.getajob.com; **www.jobbankusa.com**; **www.floridajobs.org**

Publications

How to obtain a job in the United States. Available from
www.immigrationagency.com (cost approx $60).
How to get a job in America, by Roger Jones (Howtobooks)

Starting and running a business in Florida

There are thousands of small British-run businesses in Florida (for a list see FABB, the Florida Association of British Business website **www.BritishFlorida.com**). This is one of the most well-trodden paths for foreigners to establish themselves in Florida. An E-2 Treaty Investor Visa is valid for up to five years (see Chapter 12 on Immigration into the United States).

Setting up a new business in your home country is fraught with difficulties. Most new businesses fail in the first 12 months as a result of a variety of problems associated with inexperience, lack of planning, changing market conditions and plain bad luck. A major problem is lack of liquidity or cash flow, caused by overly optimistic sales forecasts and underestimating start-up costs.

Those seeking to set up business in Florida face additional hurdles, in that you will be are operating in a foreign land in which, to begin with at least, there will be more unknowns as a result of not being in your native surroundings. For this reason a substantial number of businesses try to supply goods or services to the expatriate British or Canadian communities, including bars, local newspapers, financial advisers, estate agents, suppliers of UK food and other produce.

There are various agencies that provide help and assistance in establishing a business. Prior to arriving in Florida you could take a look at the branches of the British Chamber of Commerce in Florida (see Appendix 1). They frequently organize seminars, conferences, discussions and workshops, and are a vital source of information and contacts for those carrying out business in Florida.

In Florida you should contact the local chamber of commerce – a full list of Chambers of Commerce can be found at **www.sunnybrits.com** (go to Resources), and your local Small Business Administration Center. Take a look at Florida Trend's *Florida Small Business* magazine (available in public libraries). Ask what other help and assistance is available. In relation to exporting goods, information is available from the Division of International Trade at Enterprise Florida (see **www.eflorida.com**; tel: (305) 569 2650).

You should find a competent chartered accountant and/or commercial lawyer to advise on what form your business should take and assist with the necessary formalities. He or she can also advise you about the latest financial and other support available to businesses, and the various tax reliefs. It is vital that you choose someone with experience of doing business in Florida.

Business structures

There are four main vehicles available for the running of a business in Florida:

1. As a sole trader/proprietor. This is the easiest form of business to establish or to close down. A sole trader is personally liable for the business's debts and losses, though under Florida law the business proprietor's home is protected from creditors. Profits are taxed at the individual's federal rate of tax.

2. In partnership, where two or more people put capital into the business and share its liabilities. Partnerships are easy to establish, though it is highly advisable to enter into a written partnership agreement in which the terms are clearly set out. It is not so easy to dissolve a partnership. As for sole proprietors, the income from the business is declared on each partner's individual tax return. Again, partners remain personally liable. You do have the option of forming a limited partnership (ie a partnership with limited liability) in which case you must register with the Division of Corporations at the Florida Department of State, pay $35 to appoint a registered agent plus an additional filing fee. The filing fee starts at $52.50 and can rise to $1,750.

3. As a limited liability company (an 'LLC'). Should the business fail, the owners' liabilities are limited to the value of their shares in the company, but in practice it is likely that an owner is likely to have to give some personal guarantees, for example to the company's bank, or to its landlord if it operates from rented premises. LCCs must register with the Division of Corporations at the Florida Department of State and pay a filing fee of $125 for a new company, and thereafter $50 per year. You can choose whether the LLC is taxed as a partnership, or as a corporation.

4. As a corporation. Corporations must be incorporated with the Division of Corporations and pay a filing fee of $70. There are two types of corporation. A 'C' corporation pays its own taxes and is responsible for its own liabilities. The rate of corporation tax is 5.5 per cent. With an 'S' corporation up to 75 shareholders share the income and costs of the business and declare their shares on the individual tax returns.

The website of the Division of Corporations is **www.sunbiz.org** and that for the Internal Revenue Service is **www.irs.gov**. There are helpful explanatory leaflets that can be downloaded from the latter site. Go to **www.iris.gov/pub/irs** for those relating to partnerships (Publication 541) and corporations (Publication 542) and to **www.irs.gov/taxtopi** for sole proprietorships (Tax Topic 408).

Financial assistance: state aid and other assistance

In general there is very little in the way of grants and subsidies to assist in starting a business, save in certain cases in the high-tech sector, or in the defence industry. Details of federal grants can be found at **www.cfda.gov** and also at **www.government-grants.com**. One publication, *The Complete Guide to Government Grants* (not related in any way to the author or publisher of this book, despite its title), claims that you are certain to obtain substantial financial grants if you follow the advice it contains. It is available from **www.government-grants.org** at a cost of $30. In addition to grants to small businesses it covers home improvement, home buying, homeownership, health, education and training. There are also a variety of loan schemes that can be obtained from the US Small Business Administration.

The Florida Black Business Investment Board assists members of the black community, and more recently members of other minority communities, seeking to start up or expand an existing business by providing loans, and also offering to guarantee loans by private banks and institutions. The assistance can be anything from $20,000 to over a quarter of a million dollars. The website is **www.fbbib.com**, tel: (850) 487 4850. There is a similar body providing assistance to those with a Hispanic background.

Once a business is up and running, it may be in desperate need of venture capital to expand. One possible means of securing such investment is to contact the Florida Venture Forum (**www.fivencap.org**). It selects promising companies to make presentations at its conferences, attended by a range of investors, who provide injections of capital in return for a stake in the business.

Bank finance

Having a business plan is essential if you are to obtain a bank loan to finance your business. Indeed, this is something that you should carry out to protect the investment of your own input of capital and time. You will need to provide an assessment of the demand for your product or service and the competition, the likely revenue, the assets being introduced into the business, your fixed and variable costs and some cash flow forecasts. It is also vital that you adopt a marketing strategy – many successful businesses spend up to half their income on marketing in the first months of trading as they appreciate the importance of building a high market profile from the outset. Your plan must be based on reasonable assumptions – avoid being over-optimistic!

Ideally your business plan should be organized in a loose-leaf binder that will enable you to revise parts of the plan easily when required. It should start with a brief summary – two pages at most. This should be followed by a table of contents and sections dealing with the different issues in more detail, and finally the appendices where you can include copies of important documents or sources to which you have referred in the text of your business plan. Further guidance on putting together your business plan can be obtained from the US Small Business Administration at **www.sba.gov/starting_business/index.html**.

Other sources of assistance are the University of North Florida Small Business Development Center (see **www.sbdc.unif.edu**, tel: (904) 620 2476). The latter provides a sample business and interactive programs for writing professional business plans that you can access for a modest fee (go to 'Startingbusinessplans' on the above site).

Complying with regulations

You must ensure that you comply with the various regulations governing your business – these can be federal (ie national), state or county-level requirements. At federal level, you should file form SS-4 with the Internal Revenue Service. The IRS will then allocate a Federal Employer Identification Number (EIN) to you. This form can be downloaded from the IRS website **www.irs.gov**. Go to publications and search for IRS form SS-4. Alternatively telephone the IRS on (800) 829 4933. You will thereafter have to file quarterly federal tax returns and an annual unemployment tax return if you are an employer.

At a state level:

1. All businesses trading under a name that is not their own must register the 'fictitious' name with the Division of Corporations at the Florida Department of State. This applies even if your name is *part* of the business name. Corporations and limited partnerships are not required to do this if they are trading in their legal name, although otherwise they must. You can register online at **www.sunbiz.org**. Registrations are valid for five years and must be renewed if the name is still in use. Note that registration does not provide you with any protection for the name – it is merely to ensure that a public record is kept of who is using a fictitious name, so that users can be traced.

2. You will probably need a state business or professional licence and should enquire about this at the Florida Department of Business and Professional Regulation (see their website **www.myfloridalicense.com**, tel: (850) 487 15395).

3. You are required to collect and account for sales tax (as you would VAT in the UK), and will need to register with the Florida Department of Revenue

4. Lodge a 'New Hire Reporting Form' every time you take on a new full-time or part-time employee (for details see **www.fl-newhire.com**, tel: (888) 854 4791). This is to assist the authorities in locating parents who are avoiding paying child support, and must be carried out within 20 days of an appointment.

There may be additional obligations at a county or city level, for example in relation to building and planning regulations and the permitted use of premises, and fees payable for particular types of business use of premises. Information can be obtained from the city clerk and city building inspector, and the county tax collector and county planning department (for contact details see the Blue Pages of the local telephone directory). You should visit your local small business development centre where you can find the relevant contact details you require and information generally on the requirements of the local government bodies. A particularly useful site is **www.floridasbdc.com**. You will also find details of regulations and licensing requirements governing every conceivable activity at **www.stateofflorida.com** (go to Florida Business).

Employing others

In the United States an employer has to comply not only with national or federal regulations, governing such matters as health and safety, family and medical leave, and labour standards and equal opportunity laws, but also various state provisions. The picture is complex, and you should give serious consideration to seeking advice from a labour lawyer.

The main national provisions are the Occupational Health and Safety Act, the Fair Labor Act and the Family and Medical Care Act which fall under the auspices of the United States Department of Labour (**www.dol.gov**, tel: (866) 4872365) plus a whole range of provisions governing discrimination on the grounds of sex, race, colour, religion, national origin and disability that fall under the auspices of the Equal Employment Opportunity Commission (EEOC). See its website at **www.eeoc.gov**, and in relation to disabilities see the website **www.ada.gov**.

Employers are under a legal duty to keep their employees' workplaces safe and to keep certain health and safety records. Guidance in the form of several handbooks is available from the website of the US Department of Labour Occupational Safety and Health Administration at **www.osha.gov/dcsp/smallbusiness** – go to publications. The Fair Labor Standards Act provides that all businesses engaged in interstate business must pay a minimum wage, and that any time worked in excess of a 40-hour week must be paid at 50 per cent more than the usual hourly rate. There are strict controls on the employment of those under 16, and a prohibition on employing anyone under 18 for a range of dangerous employments. These rules apply to most employees, though there are exemptions for certain categories of employment, including white collar and computer professionals. The Family and Medical Care Act requires public sector employers and businesses employing more than 50 people to allow employees in certain circumstances leave for up to 12 weeks per year. This allows parents following the birth or adoption or fostering of a child, or a person who needs to care for a spouse, child or parent, to take leave of up to 12 weeks per year. The leave is unpaid, but the employee's job is to be protected, as is his or her entitlement to health benefits.

At a Florida level, all businesses with four or more employers must have insurance cover for workers' compensation, save that in the agricultural sector this only applies where there are five or more employees, and in the construction industry it applies to businesses with any employee. There are additional restrictions in relation to the employment of child labour. Children aged 14–15 may work up to 15 hours during school terms (up to three hours a day between 7.00 am and 7.00 pm on school days if the child is to attend school the following day and up to eight hours a day if there is no school the following day). During school holidays children aged 14 and 15 may work 40 hours a week, providing they do not work before 7.00 am and after 9.00 pm. Schoolchildren of 16 and over may work up to 30 hours a week during term, providing they start after 6.30 am and finish before 11.00 pm.

A workforce network has been created in Florida in an effort to assist small businesses taking on new employees – Employ Florida (see **www.employflorida.net**, and also **www.WorkforceFlorida.com**). It provides help in recruitment, vetting and referrals, assessing candidates' skills, training for candidates and existing employees. The Incumbent Worker Program (IWP) arranges individualized training for employees throughout Florida.

Health insurance

A number of changes have been introduced in recent years relating to health insurance, and further modifications are in the pipeline. In 2003 the Governor established an affordable health insurance task force to consider steps to improve the provision of health care in Florida, and in particular to reduce the cost of cover. As a result, a centralized health information system is being introduced to combat waste and medical errors, and steps have been introduced to facilitate the growth of the Health Savings Accounts introduced at national level. These accounts enable small employers to combine to purchase health care cover at more economical rates, and are tax deductible. The accounts are owned by individuals, and are retained by them if they change jobs or move out of the job market. It is expected that these HSAs will become increasingly popular and widespread. A list of companies that will provide health insurance to small companies is kept by the Florida Department of Financial Services and can be consulted at **www.fldfs.com/consumers**.

Insurance

It is mandatory for businesses to have insurance cover for their vehicles, health insurance for their employees and property insurance. The notification period for claims is very short. You should keep your policy document in a safe dry place that you will be able to access in the event of an emergency. You should consider carefully with the insurers the extent and level of cover that you require.

In Florida, apart from insurance for the standard risks such as buildings insurance and public liability insurance, you will need to ensure that you have cover for flood and windstorm damage. You can obtain reasonable buildings and contents insurance against flood damage from the US government's National Flood Insurance Program (**www.fema.gov/nfip**, tel: (813) 975 7451). In coastal areas, especially in the southeast and west central regions, you may find difficulty obtaining cover for windstorm damage. Wind-only policies are, however, available from the Citizens Property Insurance Corporation, **www.citizensfla.com**). Other risks that you should consider covering are business interruption to cover additional losses following flood or wind damage, insurance to cover your personal position as a director or company officer, and insurance to cover losses to the business that might be caused by the ill-health or death of a key employee. The Florida Department of Financial Services produces a

Small-Business Owner's Insurance Consumer's Guide (see their site at **www.fldfs.com** or tel: (850) 413 1601).

Taxation of businesses

In addition to corporation tax, businesses have to pay Florida's tangible tax on all assets, save real estate. Tax returns must be submitted by 1 April each year, failing which a fine is payable. The tax applies to all forms of businesses that control, manage, lease or own any tangible personal property such as furniture, equipment, computers, machines, etc.

Useful contacts

British American Business Inc: **www.babinc.org/links/jobsearch.html**
Florida Bar Lawyer Referral Service: **www.flabar.org**, tel: (800) 342 8011
US Department of Labor: **www.dol.gov**, tel: (800) 972 7332
Department of Labor Occupational Safety and Health Administration: **www.osha.gov**
Florida Small Business Development Centers: **www.floridasbdc.com**
Resource Guide: **www.800helpfla.com** – this site provides a detailed A–Z resource guide to enable you to identify the agency that you need to contact and to obtain the relevant contact details.

See also: **www.myflorida.com**; **www.oneflorida.org**; **www.sunbiz.org**; **www.myfloridalicense.com**; **www.americanbusinesslink.com**; **www.floridasmallbusiness.com**; **www.sba.gov/starting_business**.

Publications

How to start a business in the USA. Available from **www.immigrationagency.com** (cost approx $60).

14 Inheritance laws and the taxation of capital

When you purchase a property abroad, you *must* give consideration as to the effect that this is likely to have on the passing of your estate, and in particular as to how it will affect your spouse and children, or other members of your family. The law of England and Wales states that the passing of property should be in accordance with the rules of the country in which it is situated, that is, Florida, although other countries insist that property held by their nationals abroad should be distributed in accordance with the rules of their home country.

You really need to take legal advice from a lawyer with knowledge of the law in *both* your home country and Florida, and taking into account your particular circumstances and testamentary intentions.

Florida rules of succession

In Florida you are entitled to leave your estate to whomsoever you choose. There are no requirements to leave a proportion of your estate to your children (generally to the detriment of your spouse) as in France and Spain. However, if a person dies intestate (ie without making a will) his or her estate will be distributed in accordance with Florida state law which provides for distribution of your estate only to certain members of your family. Clearly, if a property (or other asset) is owned jointly, the surviving spouse will retain his or her half of the property, and the above intestacy rules will apply only to the share of the person who has died. Your estate will be managed and distributed by a court official, and the procedure will normally take longer and cost more than if you had left a will. If you have made a will in your home country, however, your estate in the United States will normally be distributed in accordance with the provision of that will if you are a non-resident at the date of your death.

Making a will

Whilst your foreign will may well be sufficient to determine how your US property should be distributed on your death, it is nevertheless preferable to have a US will, which can make your estate quicker and cheaper to manage. Furthermore, a foreign will may not have been drafted with US inheritance tax in mind, and the consequences may be rather draconian for the beneficiaries of your estate.

You should also take the opportunity of updating your existing will from your home country to take account of your testamentary plans for your Florida property. You should also note that if you emigrate to Florida, and have no remaining assets in the UK or other 'home' country, your foreign will may prove ineffective and fail to regulate the distribution of your Florida estate on your death.

Note that as in England and Wales, a Florida will is automatically revoked upon marriage, and you will need to consider making a new will.

Estate tax and tax on lifetime gifts

Those who are not resident in Florida at the time of their death pay US estate tax on the value of their US estate. As in the UK, the amount of tax is determined by the size of the total estate, and not by how much each beneficiary receives as in some continental European countries. Debts and certain expenses are deductible before arriving at the taxable value of the estate. Lifetime gifts are added to the value of the estate at death as are payments under a life policy.

The estates of non-residents (including those with non-resident visas, such as the E-2 business visa) often face hefty estate tax bills. Only the first $65,000 for non-residents is exempt from estate tax. The marginal rate of tax then gradually increases from 18 per cent up to a maximum rate of 49 per cent. On an estate valued at $100,000 the tax payable would be $24,000, on an estate of $250,000 the tax would be around $71,000, on an estate of $500,000 it would be around $155,000 and for an estate of $1 million around $250,000. For estates above $2 million every extra $1,000 attracts an additional $490 in tax. Remember that lifetime gifts have to be added to the value of the estate at death to arrive at the total tax payable. There are *partial* exemptions for transfers between husband and wife, and charitable gifts. UK citizens should note that transfers between spouses are totally exempt in the UK. Accordingly, if your spouse is the primary beneficiary under your will, you may want to keep your net assets in Florida quite low and keep most of your assets in the UK. If you expect to become a resident at some future date, and have or expect to have significant assets, it is important to discuss your plans with a financial adviser conversant with the tax systems of both Florida and your home country, in order to minimize your future tax liability.

In most cases the US estates of foreign residents will be included as part of their estate in their country of residence, and will therefore be subject to estate duties in their home country. However, in most cases (including the estates of UK and Canadian residents) the amount of US estate duty payable can be deducted from their liability to estate duty in the deceased's home country.

When the gross US estate of a non-resident is greater than $60,000 an estate tax return must be completed and filed within nine months of death.

If you are a US citizen *or* resident, the exemptions available are higher than for non-residents – currently no tax is paid on the first $1.5 million (set to rise to $2 million in 2006 and $3.5 million in 2009). On the other hand, you are liable to pay estate tax on your *worldwide* assets. Gifts to a spouse, or to a charity (and this includes a private family trust and gifts for school fees and medical expenses), are exempt. Note that if a US citizen or resident leaves his or her estate to a non-resident spouse there is no spouse exemption. The estate of a deceased should not be handled until the inheritance taxes have been paid.

Individuals are entitled to make tax-free lifetime gifts of up to $10,000 each per year to any number of beneficiaries without incurring any liability to tax.

US citizens and residents who make gifts on which tax is payable must lodge a Form 709 (Gift Tax Return) on or before 15 April of the year following the year in which the gift is made.

Wealth tax

There is currently no wealth tax in the United States, and no plans to introduce such a tax

Capital gains tax

Capital gains tax is payable whenever you sell any asset (including property, shares, personal belongings) and make a financial gain. Non-residents pay US capital gains tax on gains they make on assets sold in the US. For non-residents, gains are taxed at a standard rate of 30 per cent, though they can elect to pay tax as if they were US citizens, in which case they would pay tax at a lower rate, but on their worldwide assets. In arriving at the net gain, deductions are made for costs and taxes relating to the purchase and sale (but not interest payments). When buying property from a non-resident vendor, the buyer (or generally his or her agent or attorney) is obliged to retain 10 per cent of the sale price that he or she must pay to the IRS, and provide official proof of this payment to the vendor. The vendor then must file a tax return in order to recover any overpayment. The purchaser or his or her agent has no choice but to make this deduction – failure to do so renders the purchaser liable for the vendor's capital gains tax. It is possible to avoid this obligation by demonstrating to the authorities that the 10 per cent is higher than the tax liability, in which case they can authorize the purchaser to retain a lower amount.

You are liable to pay the tax even if you use the entire proceeds to purchase another property, that is, there is no 'rollover' of the tax. However, it is possible to defer capital gains tax on the sale of *investment* property if you exchange it for one of higher or equal value. You should obtain expert advice on the procedure necessary to benefit from this rollover provision which only covers what are termed '1031 exchanges'.

Residents pay tax on their worldwide gains. In relation to a *principal* home there is an exemption from capital gains tax on gains of up to $250,000 for a single person, and up to $500,000 for a married couple, provided the property has been owned and occupied by you for at least two of the five years prior to the sale. You are liable to pay the tax even if you use the entire proceeds of sale for the purchase of another property, that is, there is no rollover, though you can obtain rollover relief on the sale and purchase of investment properties (see paragraph above on 1031 exchanges).

The rate of capital gains tax paid by residents varies according to the period of time for which an asset is held, and the marginal rate of taxation of the person making the gain. The rates are in most cases substantially lower than the 30 per cent paid by non-residents.

Note that the estate of a deceased should not be handled until the inheritance taxes have been paid.

Appendix 1: Useful addresses

Embassies and consulates

British Embassy
3100 Massachusetts Ave, NW
Washington, DC 20008
Tel: (202) 588 6500
Fax: (202) 588 7870
www.britainusa.com

British Consulate, Miami, Florida
Brickell Bay Office Tower
1001 Brickell Bay Drive
Suite 2800
Miami, FL 33131
Tel: (305) 374 1522
Fax: (305) 374 8196
www.britainusa.com/miami

British Vice-Consulate, Orlando, Florida
Suite 2110, Sun Trust Center
200 South Orange Avenue
Orlando, FL 32801
Tel: (407) 581 1540
Fax: (407) 581 1550

Irish Embassy
2223 Massachusetts Avenue NW
Washington, DC 20008
Tel: (202) 462 3939
www.irelandemb.org

Canadian Embassy
The Embassy of Canada
501 Pennsylvania Avenue, NW
Washington, DC 20001–2114
Tel: (202) 682 1740
Fax: (202) 682 7619
E-mail: webmaster@canadianembassy.org
www.canadianembassy.org/

Canadian Consulate General Miami
Suite 1600, First Union Financial Center
200 South Biscayne Blvd
Miami, FL 33131
Tel: (305) 579 1600
Fax: (305) 374 6774
E-mail: miami-td@international.gc.ca
(For website, see **www.canadianembassy.org**, and go to Canada–US relations websites)

US embassies and consulates in the UK, Ireland and Canada

US Embassy United Kingdom
24 Grosvenor Square
London W1A 1AE.
Tel: 020 7499 9000
Visa Information Line: 09068 200 290 (24 hour) *60p/min; only available in the UK
Operator Assisted Visa Information: 09055 444 546 Mon–Fri, 8.00 am to 8.00 pm, and Sat 10.00 am to 4.00 pm; £1.30/min
www.usembassy.org.uk

US Consulate General, Belfast, Northern Ireland
Danesfort House
223 Stranmillis Road
Belfast BT9 5GR
Tel: 028 9038 6100
www.usembassy.org.uk/nireland/

US Consulate General Scotland
3 Regent Terrace
Edinburgh
Scotland EH7 5BW
Tel: 0131 556 8315
www.usembassy.org.uk/scotland/

For Wales see **www.usembassy.org.uk/wales**, tel: 02920 786633

The US embassy in London handles visa processing for Scotland and
Wales.

US Embassy Ireland
42 Elgin Road
Ballsbridge
Dublin 4
Tel: +353 1 668 8777
Fax: +353 1 668 9946
www.dublin.usembassy.gov

US Embassy Canada
490 Sussex Drive
Ottawa
Ontario K1N 1G
Tel: 613 238 5335

There are consulates in Halifax, Montreal, Quebec City, Ottawa, Toronto,
Winnipeg, Calgary and Vancouver. Their websites and details are accessible via the embassy website: **www.usembassycanada.gov**

Cultural and educational organizations

British Council
Cultural Department
British Embassy
3100 Massachusetts Avenue, NW
Washington, DC 20008–3600
Tel: 1 (202) 588 7838/6500
Fax: 1 (202) 588 7918
E-mail: educationuk.partnership@us.britishcouncil.org
www.britishcouncil.org/usa

Chambers of Commerce and Business Associations

Florida Chamber of Commerce
136 South Bronough Street
P.O. Box 11309
Tallahassee FL 32302–3309
Tel: (850) 521 1200
Fax: (850) 521 1219
E-mail: info@flchamber.com
www.flchamber.com

British-American Business Council, **www.babc.org** (over 3,500 member companies). Chapters in Miami, Orlando and Tampa:

Miami: PO Box 45 – 3306 Miami, FL 33245–3306, website: **www.baccmiami.org** (the website includes a wide collection of links to a wide range of government departments and agencies)

Orlando: PO Box 691795, Orlando, FL 32869, tel. (407) 428 6226, website: **www.baccorlando.org**

Tampa: PO Box 3447, Tampa, FL 33601–3447, tel: (813) 259 9590, E-mail: info@babctampabay.org; **www.babctampabay.org**

See also **www.britbiz.com**, a site for British individuals and companies to exchange business ideas and information. It also contains a collection of links to a variety of UK government websites.

British Food Stores

www.britishdepot.com
E-mail: service@britdepot.com
Tel: (561) 819 0204 (delivery service)

Boca Raton: The British Grocery, 6465 N. Federal Highway, Boca Raton, tel: (561) 988 0126

Fort Lauderdale: The British Depot, 1322 East Commercial Blvd, Fort Lauderdale, FL 33334, tel: (954) 491 4920

Melbourne: Lord Ravenswood Hall 909 E. New Haven Ave, Melbourne, FL 32901, tel: (321) 768 8369, **www.lordravenswoodhall.com**

Palm City: British Express, 2880 SW 42nd Avenue, Palm City, FL 34990, tel: (561) 219 0664

Sarasota: A Taste of Britain, 2236 Gulf Gate Dr, Sarasota, FL 34231, tel: (941) 927 2612

Vero Beach: The Brit Shoppe, 953 Old Dixie Hwy, Vero Beach, tel: (561) 770 1172

Canadians (information for)

Planete Quebec: **www.planete.qc.ca/floride**

Quoi faire en Floride: **www.quoifaireenfloride.net**

Natbank (subsidiary of the National Bank of Canada), tel: (954) 922 9992

Children (information for)

www.flagovkids.com
This interactive site provides information about the state of Florida, its government, history and culture in a form accessible to children.

Office of Cultural and Historical Programs
www.dos.state.fl.us/kids/history.com

Immigration (see also Chapter 12)

American Immigration Lawyers Association
918 F Street, NW
Washington, DC 20004–1400
Tel: (202) 216 2400
Fax: 202) 783 7853
www.aila.org

Peter Gold (British lawyer offering assistance with business visa and purchases): **www.emigratetotheusa.com**
Greenspoon, Marder, Hirschfeld, Rafkin, Ross & Berger attorneys (Fort Lauderdale): **www.greenspoonmarder.com**, tel: (954) 491 1120
Peter Jaensch: **www.visaamerica.com**

Information

www.stateofflorida.com – you can buy Florida residency and Florida business guides

www.myflorida.com – official portal for the state of Florida

Office of the Governor of Florida
PL 05 The Capitol
400 South Monroe Street
Tallahassee, FL 32399–1450
Tel: (850) 488 4441

Department of Business and Professional Regulation
1940 North Monroe Street
Tallahassee, FL 32399–1027
Tel: (850) 487 1395
www.myfloridalicense.com

Department of Elder Affairs
4040 Esplanade Way
Suite 315
Tallahassee FL 32399–7000
Tel: (850) 414 2000

Department of Labor and Employment Security
2012 Capital Circle
211 Hartman Building
Tallahassee, FL 32399–0685

Media

The *Union Jack* (national British newspaper with a circulation of over 200,000 containing news from Britain and information about the British in the United States) – **www.ujnews.com**

BBC America – **www.bbcamerica.com**

www.newslink.org

www.floridasmart.com – includes links to Florida's newspapers, radio and TV stations

www.tcpalm.com – links to various newspapers in Florida

www.floridatoday.com

www.news-journalonline.com

Sun-Sentinel (South Florida – covers Dade, Palm Beach and Broward)

Ft. Lauderdale Corporate Headquarters
200 E. Las Olas Blvd
Ft. Lauderdale, FL 33301
Tel: (954) 356 4000
www.sun-sentinel.com

Pubs and restaurants

Altamonte Springs: St. Andrews Tavern, 1119 W. State Road, Altamonte Springs, FL 32714, tel: (407) 788 1866

Boca Raton: Boca Blarney Stone Pub, 7200 N. Dixie Highway, Boca Raton, FL, tel: (561) 994 2818

Lion and Eagle, 2410 N. Federal Highway, Boca Raton, FL, tel: (407) 394 3190

Daniel O'Connell's Irish Pub, 51 S. E. 1st Ave., Boca Raton, FL 33432, tel: (561) 362 6484

Rayal Punjab and Bar, 1745 NW 2nd Ave, Boca Raton, FL 33432, tel: (561) 394 9898, punjabiplay@13aol.com

Jupiter: Queen Mary British Pub, Sea Plum Plaza, Military Trail/Indian Creek Parkway, Jupiter, FL 33458, **www.queenmarybritishpub.com**, **www.queenmarybritishpub.com**, **info@queenmarybritishpub.com**

Melbourne: Meg O'Malleys, 812 E. New Haven Ave., Melbourne, FL 32901, tel: (321) 952 5510

Support groups/agencies

www.britishbureau.com: health insurance, mortgages, jobs, shipping, visas, business opportunities

www.exituk.com, tel: 0208 591 7731

www.floridabritsgroup.com; **www.sunnybrits.com**; **www.flbrits.com**; **www.orlandonbritishclub.com**, **www.britishflorida.com**

Selby Corporation – advice for British citizens wishing to emigrate to Florida. **www.selby-corp.com**

info@selby-corp.com 871 W. Oakland Park Bd, Fort Lauderdale, FL 33311, tel: (954) 567 0577

Tourist information

Visit Florida: **www.flausa.com**

Florida Attractions Association, PO Box 10295, Tallahassee, FL 32302, tel: (850) 222 2885

Parks: Department of Environmental Protection, Office of Recreation and Parks Mail Station, 5353900 Commonwealth Bd, Tallahassee, FL 32399–3000, tel: (850) 488 9872, **www.dep.state.fl.us/parks**

Historical sites: Division of Historical Resources, Florida Department of State, R.A. Gray Building 500 S. Bronough St., Tallahassee, FL 32399–0250, **www.dos.state.fl.us**

Sports: Florida Sports Foundation, 2964 Wellington Circle of North Tallahassee, FL 32308, tel: (850) 488 8347

Camping sites: Florida Association of RV Parks and Campgrounds, 1340 Vickers Dr., Tallahassee, FL 32303, tel: (850) 562 7151, **www.florida-camping.com**

Hotels: Florida Hotel and Motel Association, PO Box 1529, Tallahassee, FL 32302, tel: (850) 224 2888

Appendix 2:
Travel by air to Florida

Florida has six international airports: Miami, Orlando, Tampa/St. Petersburg, Fort Lauderdale, Jacksonville and Daytona Beach. Miami airport is one of the main gateways into the USA, and the main gateway from South and Central American and the Caribbean. It has the drawback that delays at immigration and customs controls can be very time-consuming.

There are relatively few direct scheduled flights from the UK or Europe, although there are some direct flights to Miami, Orlando and Tampa. There are many flights with one change, often in New York, Newark or Washington, DC. There are direct flights to Florida destinations from Toronto and Vancouver, and other cities in Canada.

The budget airline Globespan flies direct to Toronto from Belfast, Birmingham, Edinburgh, Exeter, Glasgow, Manchester, Newcastle, Dublin and Shannon and it may be worthwhile considering flying to Florida via Toronto.

There is a good selection of charter flights from UK airports to Miami, Orlando and Tampa.

Daytona Beach International Airport
www.flydaytonafirst.com

Fort Lauderdale Hollywood International Airport
www.broward.org/airport
Direct flights to Canada and the Caribbean, but not Europe.
Broward County. Reasonable drive from Fort Lauderdale and Miami.
Tel: 1 (954) 359 1200

Jacksonville International Airport
www.jaa.aero

Miami International Airport
customerservice@miami-airport.com
Over 100 airlines flying to around 150 destinations worldwide.
Tel: 1 (305) 876 7000
The airport has a 24-hour voice-activated telephone hotline: (305) 876 7000

Orlando International Airport
www.orlandoairports.net
Flights to London and Manchester (BMI, BA, Virgin Atlantic), Amsterdam
and seven major airports in Canada: Winnipeg, Calgary, Toronto,
Montreal, Ottawa, Hamilton, Halifax.

Orlando Sandford International Airport
www.orlandosandfordairport.com
Flights to North, South and Central America. Tel: 1 (407) 585 400
Eighteen miles north of Orlando.

The following charter airlines have flights into Orlando Sandford
International Airport: Monarch Airlines, Britannia Airways, Air
Atlanta, Air Scandic, Avia Jet, My Travel, First Choice, Travel City Direct,
Thomas Cook. The websites of all these airlines are accessible via
www.orlandosandfordairport.com – go to airlines and scroll down to
International Charters. No scheduled flights to the UK or Europe.

Tampa International Airport
www.tampaairport.com
Direct flights to London GTW (US Airlines), Toronto (Air Canada)

Other airports

Key West International Airport
www.keywestinternationalairport.com

Melbourne Airport
www.mlbair.com
info@mlbair.com

Palm Beach International Airport
www.pbia.org – flights to London GTW and HRW, Birmingham,
Manchester and Dublin all involving one change. Flights to Montreal and
Toronto both involve one change.

Panama City Bay County International Airport
www.pcairport.com

Pensacola Regional Airport
www.flypensacola.com
Tel: 1 (850) 436 5005
Services include flights to Atlanta, Houston, Orlando, Charlotte, Tampa,
Miami.

Sarasota-Bradenton International Airport
www.srq-airport.com
Tel: 1 (941) 359 2770
Direct flights to Toronto and Ottawa.

South West Florida International Airport
www.flylcpa.com
Flights to Manchester and London, also Calgary, Montreal, Toronto,
Quebec and Winnipeg with one change only.

St. Petersburg Clearwater International Airport
www.fly2pie.com
Direct flights to Toronto, Hamilton, Ontario, Halifax, Nova Scotia, St.
John's, Newfoundland.

Tallahassee Regional Airport
www.state.fl.us/citytlh/aviation
Tel: 1 (850) 891 7802
Flights to Manchester, London, Dublin, Glasgow with one change. Flights
to Calgary, Hamilton, Ontario, Montreal, Toronto, Quebec all with one
change.

Details of all commercial airports throughout Florida can be found on
www.myflorida.com and **www.florida.worldweb.com/Transportation/
Airports**.

Airlines

Air France	**www.airfrance.co.uk**	Tel: 0845 082 0162
Air Transit	**www.athusa.com**	
American	**www.aa.com**	Tel: 0845 778 9789
British Airways	**www.britishairways.com**	Tel: 0845 773 3377
BMI	**www.flybmi.com**	Tel: 0870 607 0555
Canjet	**www.canjet.com**	
Continental	**www.continental.com**	Tel: 0800 776 464
Delta	**www.delta.com**	Tel: 0800 414 767
Sunwing	**www.sunwing.ca**	
US Airways	**www.usairways.com**	Tel: 0845 600 3300
Virgin Atlantic	**www.virgin-atlantic.com**	Tel: 0871 222 3767
United Airlines	**www.unitedairlines.co.uk**	Tel: 0845 844 4777

Regional airlines

Gulf Stream	**www.gulfstreamair.com**
Southeast Airlines	**www.southeastairfares.com**

Appendix 3:
Pet travel scheme – approved routes and carriers to the United States

By sea

New York City	Southampton	Cunard Line

By air

Atlanta or Houston	London Gatwick	BA (accompanied animals only)
Boston or Miami	London Heathrow	American Airlines Cargo, BA, Virgin Atlantic
Chicago	London Heathrow	American Airlines Cargo, BA
Newark	London Gatwick	Continental Airlines (accompanied animals only)
New York (JFK)	London Heathrow	American Airlines Cargo, BA, Virgin Atlantic
New York (JFK)	Manchester	BA (accompanied animals only)
Orlando	London Gatwick	Virgin Atlantic (accompanied animals only)
Sandford	London Gatwick	Britannia Airways, Excel Airways, My Travel (accompanied animals only on all airlines)

Sanford	Manchester	Britannia Airways, Excel Airways, My Travel (accompanied animals only on all airlines)

The above information is subject to variation, so you should check before making your travel plans. Pets travel as cargo, though on a small number of flights guide dogs are permitted in the cabin. See the DEFRA website (details below).

Information

Pets Helpline
Tel: 08459 33557 (Monday–Friday, 8.30 am to 5.00 pm, UK time)
www.defra.gov.uk
E-mail: helpline@defra.gsi.gov.uk

Appendix 4: Clothes sizes

Women (coats, dresses, skirts)

UK	8	10	12	14	16	18	20	22
US	6	8	10	12	14	16	18	20

Women (blouses and jumpers)

UK	31	32	34	36	38	40	42 (inches)
US	6	8	10	12	14	16	18 (size)

Women (shoes)

UK	3.5	4/4.5	5	5.5	6	6.5	7
US	5	5.5/6	6.5	7	7.5	8	8.5

Men (shoes)

UK	6	7	8	9	10	11	12
US	7	8	9	10	11	12	13

Children (clothes)

UK	16/18	20/22	24/26	28/30	32/34	36/38
US	2	4	6	8	10	12

Children (shoes)

UK	2	3	4	4.5	5	6	7	7.5	8	9
US	2	3	4	4.5	5	6	7	7.5	8	9
UK	10	11	11.5	12	13	1	2	2.5	3	4
US	10	11	11.5	12	13	1	2	2.5	3	4

Appendix 5: Public holidays

1 January	New Year's Day
3rd Monday in January	Martin Luther King Day
3rd Monday in February	The President's Day
Easter Sunday	
Easter Monday	
4th Monday in May	Memorial Day
4 July	Independence Day
1st Monday in September	Labour Day
2nd Monday in October	Columbus Day
11 November	Veterans' Day
4th Thursday in November	Thanksgiving Day
25 December	Christmas Day

Index

Index of advertisers